BRAIN GAMES®

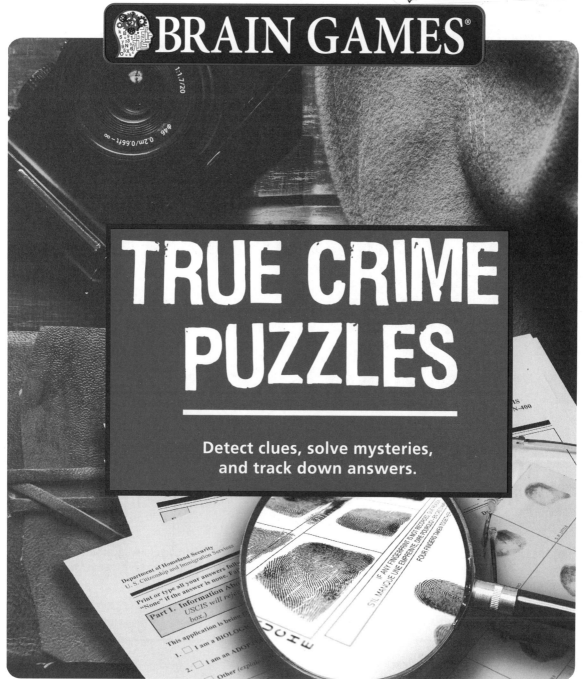

TRUE CRIME PUZZLES

Detect clues, solve mysteries,
and track down answers.

Publications International, Ltd.

Puzzles created by: Stephen Ryder and Nicole Sulgit

Puzzles illustrated by: Brent Saemann and Nicole Sulgit

Images from: Shutterstock.com

Louis Weber, CEO
Publications International, Ltd.
8140 Lehigh Avenue
Morton Grove, IL 60053

ISBN: 978-1-64030-272-3

Manufactured in U.S.A.

8 7 6 5 4 3 2 1

CAN YOU DEDUCE THE SOLUTIONS?

Do you know the names and stories of Borden, Burke, and Barrow? Do you thrill to the stories of heists, poisonings, and mobsters? Do you think you have the eagle eyes and keen mind of a dogged investigator? If so, then *Brain Games®: True Crime Puzzles* is the book for you.

Some of the puzzles in this collection revisit well-known historical crimes and criminals, from an Al Capone word search to a memory puzzle involving John Wilkes Booth's conspirators. Other puzzles, including cryptograms and matching puzzles, might introduce some stories that are new to you. From a jewel theft in 1600s England to an armored car heist not too long ago, *Brain Games®: True Crime Puzzles* presents a variety of crimes—and a variety of puzzles. But don't stop there. Test your own investigative acumen against visual puzzles that ask you spot changes in crime scenes, logic puzzles that ask you to deduce the truth from a given set of clues, and more.

Don't worry if you find yourself getting stuck from time to time. Answers are found at the back of the book when you need a helpful boost. So grab your pencil, dust off your knowledge of D.B. Cooper and Thomas Blood, and start searching for clues.

Every word listed is contained within the group of letters. Words can be found in a straight line horizontally, vertically, or diagonally. They may be read either forward or backward.

ALCATRAZ

ALPHONSE

BOOTLEGGING

BUGS MORAN

CHICAGO OUTFIT

CICERO

FIVE POINTS GANG

JOHNNY TORRIO

ORGANIZED CRIME

PINEAPPLE PRIMARY

PUBLIC ENEMY

RACKETEERING

SCARFACE

ST. VALENTINE DAY MASSACRE

SYPHILIS

TAX EVASION

WILLIAM HALE THOMPSON

```
H Q O F D J D H R A C K E T E E R I N G R Q Y
S W F I X N U I H H L B T Y I S U H A E T O R
G X O D Q C J G Q I E Y A H K S O F I Y P F A
N L X S G K S N V X M C I H M P H G O X E L M
I E G D N C R A D X I Y R T T K G B W U P V I
G I T L A S T R N G R A L C A T R A Z B B V R
G C L I G H W O Z O C L Z U M T Z D G R R Q P
E R C A S S A M Y A D E N I T N E L A V T S E
L C S O T Y S S A N E T P F O N T J N S U X L
T X P C N M N G G D Z T J V E H I R S Y F V P
O A N M I E J U S T I Q X P L E F G R L V Z P
O S A K O N H B Z Y N K M L V T T Z S N R S A
B I Q U P E C A Z N A X N H O T U D C O Q Z E
T K K W E C D A Q S G J T I T R O U A I A S N
G M L A V I Y G O N R R B O F A O U R S K I I
S A U Q I L R Z W L O C R M R Q G F F A T L P
B E D C F B F D Z F O T I T Q E A A A V E I W
U X N B V U G X R Q L I K M P Q C B C E Q H G
R T A S L P H X H G I V H G H Y I I E X C P J
T S Y G L P Q K P C W N F M H Q H Z C A T Y I
H Q E S N O H P L A U N C R Z B C W F T O S I
J M N J O H N N Y T O R R I O I Z I G H Q W U
W I L L I A M H A L E T H O M P S O N U R T R
```

5

Answers on page 172.

Read this true crime account, then turn to the next page to test your knowledge.

It was a terrible thing to wake up to on that March morning in 1927. Nine-year-old Lorraine Snyder found her mother Ruth, her hands and feet bound, begging for help in the hall outside her bedroom. The girl rushed to her neighbors in the New York City suburb, and they called the police.

What the police found was more terrible still. Ruth Snyder's husband Albert lay dead in the bedroom—his skull smashed, wire strung around his neck, and a chloroform-soaked cloth shoved up his nose. His 32-year-old widow told the police that a large Italian man had knocked her out, stolen her jewelry, and assaulted her husband.

But the police found her jewels under a mattress; they also discovered a bloody pillowcase and a bloody, five-pound sash weight in a closet. As if this evidence wasn't damning enough, police located a check Ruth had written to Henry Judd Gray in the amount of $200. Gray's name was found in her little black book—along with the names of 26 other men. Little Lorraine told the cops that "Uncle Judd" had been in the home the previous night. A tie clip with the initials HJG was found on the floor.

The marriage had been unhappy for some time. Ruth Brown met Albert Snyder—14 years her senior—in 1915. He was an editor of *Motor Boating* magazine, and Ruth was a secretary. She and Albert married and had Lorraine, but their union was flawed from the start. Albert was still enthralled with his former fiancée of ten years ago, who had died; he named his boat after her and displayed her photograph in his and Ruth's home.

In the meantime, Ruth haunted the jazz clubs of Roaring Twenties Manhattan, drinking and dancing 'til the wee hours of the morning without her retiring spouse, whom she had dubbed "the old crab." In 1925, the unhappy wife went on a blind date and met Judd Gray, a low-key corset salesperson. Soon the duo was meeting for afternoon trysts at the Waldorf-Astoria—leaving Lorraine to play in the hotel lobby. Eventually, Ruth arranged for her unsuspecting husband to sign a life insurance policy worth more than $70,000.

At the murder scene, the police questioned Ruth about Gray. "Has he confessed?," she blurted. It wasn't long before she had spilled her guts, though she claimed it was Gray who'd actually strangled Albert. Meanwhile, 33-year-old Gray—not exactly the sharpest knife in the drawer—was found at a hotel in Syracuse, New York. It didn't take police long to locate him; after leaving Ruth's house, he had actually stopped to ask a police officer when he could catch the next bus to New York City. Gray quickly confessed but claimed it was Ruth who'd strangled Albert.

A month after the arrest of the murderous duo, a brief trial ensued. For three weeks, the courtroom was jammed with 1,500 spectators. Ruth was given the moniker "The Blonde Butcher." In attendance were such luminaries as songwriter Irving Berlin and the novelist James M. Cain, who drew on the case for his novel *Double Indemnity*. The media frenzy over the courtroom drama even exceeded coverage of the execution of anarchist-bombers Sacco and Vanzetti. Miming the fevered reporting of city tabloids such as *The Daily News,* the stodgy *New York Times* carried page-one stories on the crime for months.

Ruth and Gray were pronounced guilty after a 100-minute deliberation by an all-male jury. When their appeal failed and their plea for clemency to Governor Al Smith was denied, the deadly pair was driven 30 miles "up the river" to Sing Sing Prison's death row. En route, excited onlookers hung from rooftops to catch a glimpse of the doomed couple. The pair were executed on January 12, 1928, by the electric chair. At the instant of execution, a reporter for the *Daily News* triggered a camera hidden in his pants. A garish photo of the murderess's last moment would appear on the paper's front page the next day. The headline read, "DEAD."

Minutes later, it was Gray's turn. Although his feet caught fire during the execution, for most witnesses it was Ruth's final moments that were stamped indelibly in their minds.

(Do not read this until you have read the previous page!)

1. The first name of the victim was:
   A. Albert
   B. Alfred
   C. Alphonse
   D. Snyder

2. Judd Gray left this behind at the murder scene:
   A. A pair of cufflinks with his initials
   B. A tie clip with his initials
   C. A pair of shoes
   D. An engraved pen

3. Ruth was called by this nickname.
   A. The Ruthless Widow
   B. Black Widow
   C. The Blonde Butcher
   D. The Murderess

4. This newspaper captured a photograph of the execution.
   A. *The Daily News*
   B. The *New York Times*
   C. The *New York Post*
   D. The *Daily Tribune*

Answers on page 172

Cryptograms are messages in substitution code. Break the code to read the message. For example, THE SMART CAT might become FVO QWGDF JGF if **F** is substituted for **T, V** for **H, O** for **E,** and so on.

BXOOX QGZ FLQGC BQEXO BHAGXZ PNX KRQGPLADD LQAZXLO JQGJ AG PNXAL PXXG VXQLO QGZ WXJQG PNXAL DAFXOPVDX HF WQGC QGZ PLQAG LHWWXLV. BXOOX'O EHPNXL YXLXDZQ TLHPX Q WHHC QFPXL NAO ZXQPN TAPN PNX ZXZAMQPAHG: "AG DHSAGJ EXEHLV HF EV WXDHSXZ OHG, ERLZXLXZ WV Q PLQAPHL QGZ MHTQLZ TNHOX GQEX AO GHP THLPNV PH QIIXQL NXLX."

Answers on page 172.

Bremleytown's Animal Control Center has had a busy week! Five different citations were levied by the local authorities against people who were keeping illegal pets in their residences. Using only the clues below, match each law-breaking pet owner to his or her street location, and determine the type of animal they owned and the day on which Animal Control picked it up.

1. The Animal Control team showed up at Edith Estes's door sometime before they picked up the bear cub.

2. Gil Gates had his illegal pet (which wasn't the bear cub) taken away 2 days before the visit to Kirk Lane.

3. The skunk was either the animal picked up on August 7th or the one that was being kept on Walnut Avenue.

4. Animal Control stopped by Walnut Avenue three days before they picked up the wolf on Island Road (which didn't belong to Flora Flynn).

5. Iva Ingram had her pet taken away 3 days before the anaconda was captured. She didn't live on Post Street.

	Owners					Streets					Animals				
	Abe Alvarez	Edith Estes	Flora Flynn	Gil Gates	Iva Ingram	Green Blvd.	Island Rd.	Kirk Ln.	Post St.	Walnut Ave.	Anaconda	Bear cub	Cheetah	Skunk	Wolf
Dates August 4															
August 5															
August 6															
August 7															
August 8															
Animals Anaconda															
Bear cub															
Cheetah															
Skunk															
Wolf															
Streets Green Blvd.															
Island Rd.															
Kirk Ln.															
Post St.															
Walnut Ave.															

Dates	Owners	Streets	Animals
August 4			
August 5			
August 6			
August 7			
August 8			

Answers on page 172.

MOTEL HIDEOUT

A thief hides out in one of the 45 motel rooms listed in the chart below. The motel's in-house detective received a sheet of four clues, signed "The Logical Thief." Using these clues, the detective found the room number within 15 minutes—but by that time, the thief had fled. Can you find the thief's motel room quicker?

1. The sum of the digits is less than 6.

2. The first digit is not 4.

3. The second digit is not 2.

4. It is divisible by 2.

51	52	53	54	55	56	57	58	59
41	42	43	44	45	46	47	48	49
31	32	33	34	35	36	37	38	39
21	22	23	24	25	26	27	28	29
11	12	13	14	15	16	17	18	19

Answers on page 173

Read the story below, than turn the page and answer the questions.

The detective overheard the jewelry thief tell her accomplice about the different places where she stashed the loot. She said, "Two of the diamonds are taped underneath a loose floorboard in the master bedroom. The other three are taped to the light fixture in the bathroom. The pearls are in a can of cornmeal in the kitchen. The gold bars are behind the laundry machine in the basement."

(Do not read this until you have read the previous page!)

The investigator overheard the information about where the stolen loot was stored, but didn't have anywhere to write it down! Answer the questions below to help the investigator remember.

1. How many diamonds are there altogether?
   - A. 2
   - B. 3
   - C. 4
   - D. 5

2. Some of the diamonds are taped to a light fixture in this room.
   - A. Master bedroom
   - B. Bathroom
   - C. Kitchen
   - D. Basement

3. What is found in the basement?
   - A. Gold bars
   - B. Gold coins
   - C. Pearls
   - D. Diamonds

4. The pearls are found in a can of this.
   - A. Baking powder
   - B. Oatmeal
   - C. Cornmeal
   - D. Baking soda

Answers on page 173.

On Baldwin Avenue, there are 5 houses that are identical to each other. You need to follow up with a witness, Joanna Winchell, but without any address on the doors you are not sure which house to approach. You know that Winchell is a single mom and that her daughter Sophie owns a cat. The staff at the ice cream shop around the corner and your own observations give you some clues. From the information given, can you find the right house?

A. Only two children live full-time on the street, and they live next door to each other.

B. The divorced man in house D has custody of his kids ever other weekend.

C. The people in both corner houses have dogs, not cats.

D. Sophie used to come into the ice cream shop with her next door neighbor and babysitter Hannah, but Hannah is off at college now, and her parents are thinking of moving to a smaller place for "empty nesters."

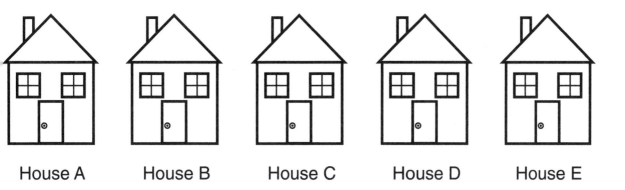

House A   House B   House C   House D   House E

Answers on page 173.

STOLEN ART

Each piece of artwork listed below has been stolen, and only some have been recovered. Every piece of artwork listed is contained within the group of letters. Words can be found in a straight line horizontally, vertically, or diagonally. They may be read either forward or backward.

CHEZ TORTONI (Édouard Manet)

THE CONCERT (Johannes Vermeer)

FEMME ASSISE (Henri Matisse)

LANDSCAPE WITH COTTAGES (Rembrandt van Rijn)

MONA LISA (Leonardo da Vinci)

LE PIGEON AUX PETITS POIS (Pablo Picasso)

PORTRAIT OF A LADY (Gustav Klimt)

POPPY FLOWERS (Vincent van Gogh)

SAINT JEROME WRITING (Caravaggio)

THE SCREAM (Edvard Munch)

SELF-PORTRAIT (Rembrandt van Rijn)

WATERLOO BRIDGE, LONDON (Claude Monet)

```
P S U F S S G L P B R F E B D B L T Z P W
T I I M A E W G Z J Y S R F K M N V D A W
N O P N Z G A Q K R X E H G A V A F B R V
N P S N O A T P J M H H X E V O E J R A P
E S A O K T E C D Q D G R I H Q W P S Y K
P T I N C T R T Q K R C W I E G O I Y Y S
O I N P P O L O J W S Z U L W D L J Q R S
R T T L C C O J T E D D W O T A Y F E H E
T E J X L H O A H Z F B Q M N V O W N I L
R P E K Y T B T O T E E Y O Y U O V T Q F
A X R E H I R T C S M H M G G L K R Y X P
I U O C A W I K P U Y L C M F E E I B X O
T A M S K E D C N A I F U Y E C N X D G R
O N E D M P G X X R E A P C N A W T G H T
F O W N T A E Z Q T F P P O Y L S K Y V R
A E R M D C L P Y E O Q C R R A R S W L A
L G I A E S O Z T P I E T E X Q C G I B I
A I T A I D N X D Z H F J J S F Z W W S T
D P I B A N D N F T G U Q C Y B V R O W E
Y E N P Y A O Q L I K S G R B P K O K C B
H L G E A L N V S B H H T Z Z Z Q H J C A
```

Answers on page 173.

Change just one letter on each line to go from the top word to the bottom word. Do not change the order of the letters. You must have a common English word at each step.

CLUE

_____

_____

_____

_____

_____

_____

RAID

Answers on page 173.

Read this true crime account, then turn to the next page to test your knowledge.

In 1905, when the police finally caught up with Johann Hoch, he had already proposed to what would have been his 45th wife. Born in 1855 in Germany, Hoch eventually immigrated to the United States. His habit was to meet a lonely middle-aged woman, propose, marry her, and take her money in the space of about a week. Depending on Johann's mood, about a third of the women were murdered; the others were simply abandoned.

Hoch's method of murder was slipping his new bride some arsenic, which was a perfect crime in those days. Arsenic was used in embalming fluid, so the minute an undertaker came into the house, convicting someone of arsenic poisoning was impossible.

The press was fascinated—how could an ugly man who spoke like a comedian with a German accent convince so many women to marry him? Why, his last wife from Chicago (his 44th overall) had agreed to marry him while her sister (wife #43) was lying dead on her bed! *The Herald American,* which could be counted on to print the wildest rumors in town, claimed that Hoch used hypnosis on the women and that he had learned all he knew about murdering from the infamous H. H. Holmes.

Hoch's power over women made it seem as though he *must* have had access to some sort of magic spell. As his trial continued, wife #44, the woman who had first reported him to authorities, came to his cell daily to bring him money and beg him to forgive her. He received numerous letters containing marriage proposals while in prison. Any marriage would have been a short one—Johann was hanged in 1906.

Legend has it that as Hoch was about to be hanged, he said to the guards, "I don't look like a monster now, do I?" After the deed was done, one of the guards quietly replied, "Well, not anymore."

(Do not read this until you have read the previous page!)

1. Johann Hoch murdered all his wives.

_____ True

_____ False

2. Hoch's preferred method of murder was this.

A. Arsenic

B. Rat poison

C. Suffocation

D. Strangulation

3. Hoch received marriage proposals while in prison.

_____ True

_____ False

4. Hoch married at least this many women.

A. 20

B. 30

C. 40

D. 100

Answers on page 174.

Study this picture of the crime scene for 1 minute, then turn the page.

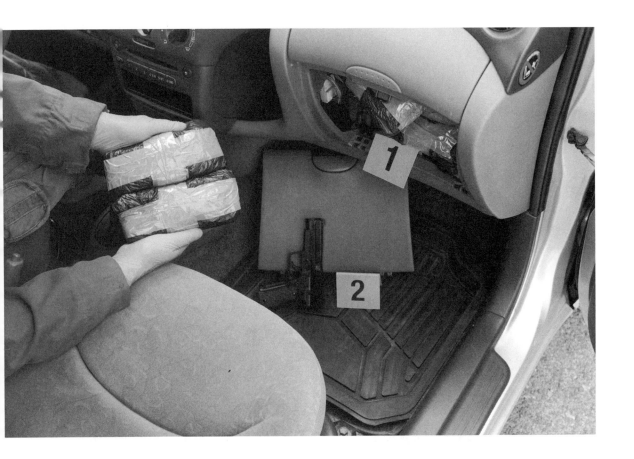

(Do not read this until you have read the previous page!) Which image exactly matches the crime scene?

1.

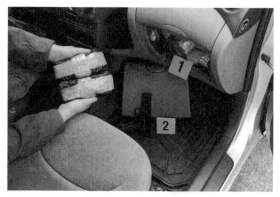

2.

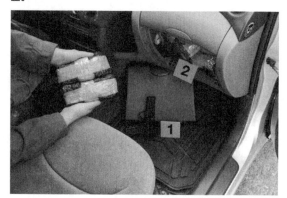

3.

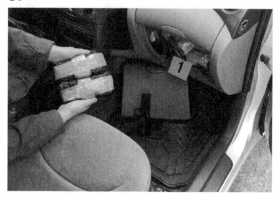

4.

Answers on page 174.

Read this true crime account, then turn to the next page to test your knowledge.

The U.S. Department of Justice reports that fewer than 5 percent of all bank robbers are women and that women involved in bank robberies are more likely to be accomplices than ringleaders. But there are some interesting stories out there. Statistics indicate that the average amount of money taken from any bank heist is less than $5,000, leaving psychologists to wonder if the motivating factor is love, money, or adventure.

For a short two-year period, 1932–34, Bonnie Parker and Clyde Barrow captivated the nation by posing as that generation's Romeo and Juliet—on the lam from the law. Credited with 13 murders and countless robberies, it is thought that Clyde and his "Barrow Gang" actually committed most of the crimes. Some in the gang claimed they never saw Bonnie fire a gun, even if she was frequently photographed brandishing weapons and self-parodying the gangster image. She also immortalized their legend by writing "The Story of Bonnie & Clyde," which she sent to the media. Their crime spree took them across several states, but the law finally caught up to them outside of Sailes, Louisiana, where the pair was killed in a gunfight.

Not quite as famous was Monica "Machine Gun Molly" Proietti from Quebec, Canada. A tiny woman of less than 100 pounds, Proietti was involved in more than 20 bank robberies during the 1960s, leading an all-male band of criminals. She was gunned down at age 27 after she and two accomplices robbed a bank and made off with $3,074.

In 2003, Naomi Betts robbed the Fifth Third Bank in Indianapolis, Indiana, and was arrested about six months later after an airing of *America's Most Wanted* on TV. During the robbery, she didn't even attempt to conceal her face.

Accomplices of other famous bank robbers include: Etta Place, lover of Harry "The Sundance Kid" Longbaugh; Mary Katherine Haroney, aka Big Nose Kate, companion of Doc Holliday; and Kate "Ma" Barker, who shielded her sons and hid their crimes for years.

(Do not read this until you have read the previous page!)

1. About this percentage of bank robbers are women.
    A. 1%
    B. 5%
    C. 15%
    D. 45%

2. Bonnie's last name was:
    A. Parker
    B. Clyde
    C. Barrow
    D. Barker

3. Monica Proietti's nickname was:
    A. Big Nose
    B. Ma
    C. Machine Gun Monica
    D. Machine Gun Molly

4. Proietti was active in this decade.
    A. 1920s
    B. 1940s
    C. 1960s
    D. 1980s

Answers on page 174.

Read the story below, than turn the page and answer the questions.

The detective overheard the jewelry thief tell his accomplice about the different places where he stashed the loot. He said, "The sapphire is tucked in a running shoe in the spare closet. The diamond necklace is behind the mirror in the dining room. The ruby is at the bottom of the salt shaker. The emeralds are in a waterproof bag in the toilet tank."

(Do not read this until you have read the previous page!)

The investigator overheard the information about where the stolen loot was stored, but didn't have anywhere to write it down! Answer the questions below to help the investigator remember.

1. The sapphire is found in this location.
   A. The toe of a slipper
   B. The toe of a running shoe
   C. The bottom of the salt shaker
   D. In the refrigerator

2. What is found behind the mirror in the dining room?
   A. The sapphire
   B. The diamond ring
   C. The diamond necklace
   D. The emeralds

3. How many emeralds are there?
   A. 1
   B. 2
   C. 3
   D. We are not told.

4. What kind of gem is found in the salt shaker?
   A. Sapphire
   B. Diamond
   C. Ruby
   D. Emerald

Answers on page 174.

MOTEL HIDEOUT

A thief hides out in one of the 45 motel rooms listed in the chart below. The motel's in-house detective received a sheet of four clues, signed "The Logical Thief." Using these clues, the detective found the room number within 15 minutes—but by that time, the thief had fled. Can you find the thief's motel room quicker?

1. It is not divisible by 5.

2. It is divisible by 3.

3. The first digit is larger than the second.

4. The second digit is greater than 2.

51	52	53	54	55	56	57	58	59
41	42	43	44	45	46	47	48	49
31	32	33	34	35	36	37	38	39
21	22	23	24	25	26	27	28	29
11	12	13	14	15	16	17	18	19

27

Answers on page 174.

Every word listed is contained within the group of letters. Words can be found in a straight line horizontally, vertically, or diagonally. They may be read either forward or backward.

ABDUCTIONS

CBS

COLD CASES

DENNIS FARINA

DOCUMENTARY

EYEWITNESS

HOTLINE

INTERVIEW

LIFETIME

MISSING PERSONS

NBC

REENACTMENT

ROBERT STACK

SPIKE

UPDATES

VIRGINIA MADSEN

WANTED

```
R A I H S M Z E O R F J C R W U V A S
F F X X U A E K C F F C K E J X D C B
B D Q D M B K C A T S T R E B O R J C
S N W R A W Y D H A U M M N D N S D B
N S E D V K L J O S U I M A R M Q W Z
O I R S F S L Y E C T X O C Q U S R D
S B X Z D P M S A E U H O T L I N E K
R M U S E A A N F B S M N M X W A R S
E P J D S C M I F D D M E E C I D E C
P N S S D E L A I E K U A N N V T Y D
G A M L I G N G I T J K C T T A R E M
N P O P Q K E T V N O E E T D A A O G
I C L Q E N A C I A I R S P I Y R U A
S U R O K N M C Q W V G U E E O D Y H
S Y W N I V B L Y I E B R A Y X N U R
I A U M P J O C E B H Y R I K H T S R
M Z T K S J W W V C J J E Y V B S T D
D E N N I S F A R I N A Y U N L Y D Z
F B V D S O B W F O X E F Z V F D P O
```

Answers on page 175.

Cryptograms are messages in substitution code. Break the code to read the message. For example, THE SMART CAT might become FVO QWGDF JGF if **F** is substituted for **T, V** for **H, O** for **E,** and so on.

AQXEAXG LIAOIGPN BRAEAX QIVXGX EASPK AG QJP

1600O. OJP KPSPEILPK X LIAOIG YXEEPK XMRX QIVXGX

XGK OIEK AQ QI TIFPG EIIDAGB QI FRNKPN QJPAN

JROHXGKO. TJPG QJP LIEAYP YXFP VIN JPN, OJP

VEPK XGK OIRBJQ OXGYQRXNW AG X YJRNYJ; EIYXEO

BNXQPVRE VIN JPN LNPSAIRO JPEL LNIQPYQPK JPN.

PSPGQRXEEW, JITPSPN, OJP TXO XNNPOQPK XGK

PUPYRQPK, XEIGB TAQJ JPN KXRBJQPN XGK OPSPNXE

IQJPN XYYIFLEAYPO.

Answers on page 175.

Study this picture of the crime scene for 1 minute, then turn the page.

(Do not read this until you have read the previous page!) Which image exactly matches the picture from the previous page?

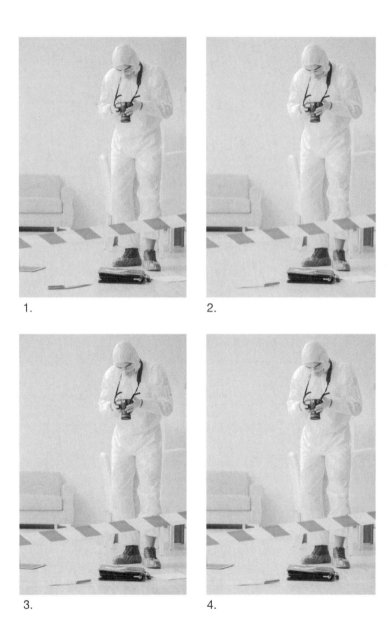

1.

2.

3.

4.

Answers on page 175.

Study this picture of the crime scene for 1 minute, then turn the page.

(Do not read this until you have read the previous page!) Which image exactly matches the crime scene?

1.

2.

3.

4.

Answers on page 175

Read the story below, than turn the page and answer the questions.

The detective overheard the thief tell his accomplice about the different places where he stashed the loot. He said, "I left the jewels at the apartment on 4th Street, the gold bars at the condo on 48th Street, the $235,000 in unmarked bills in a safety deposit box at the bank on Pearson Avenue, and the art forgery at the townhome on Reardon Street."

(Do not read this until you have read the previous page!)

The investigator overheard the information about where the stolen loot was stored, but didn't have anywhere to write it down! Answer the questions below to help the investigator remember.

1. The jewels are found on this street.
   A. 4th Street
   B. 48th Street
   C. Pearson Avenue
   D. Reardon Street

2. The gold bars are found in this type of building.
   A. Apartment
   B. Condo
   C. Townhome
   D. Office

3. How much money did the thief stash?
   A. $205,000
   B. $215,000
   C. $225,000
   D. $235,000

4. What is found on Reardon Street?
   A. Jewels
   B. Gold bars
   C. Unmarked bills
   D. Art forgery

Answers on page 176

MOTEL HIDEOUT

A thief hides out in one of the 45 motel rooms listed in the chart below. The motel's in-house detective received a sheet of four clues, signed "The Logical Thief." Using these clues, the detective found the room number within 15 minutes—but by that time, the thief had fled. Can you find the thief's motel room quicker?

1. It is a prime number.

2. It is less than 40.

3. The sum of the digits is greater than 8.

4. The second digit is less than nine.

51	52	53	54	55	56	57	58	59
41	42	43	44	45	46	47	48	49
31	32	33	34	35	36	37	38	39
21	22	23	24	25	26	27	28	29
11	12	13	14	15	16	17	18	19

Answers on page 176.

THE FATTY ARBUCKLE SCANDAL

Early Hollywood had its share of scandals. In the 1920s, Rocsoe Conkling "Fatty" Arbuckle was accused of the murder of Virginia Rappe. After two hung juries, in a third trial, he was acquitted of all charges. Every word listed is contained within the group of letters. Words can be found in a straight line horizontally, vertically, or diagonally. They may be read either forward or backward.

ACQUITTAL

ACTOR

ARBUCKLE

BUSTER KEATON (friend of the actor)

CHARLIE CHAPLIN (friend of the actor)

COMEDIAN

CONKLING

EXONERATION

HOLLYWOOD

HUNG JURIES

MANSLAUGHTER

MAUDE DELMONT (Rappe's friend, Arbuckle's accuser)

PARAMOUNT

ROSCOE

SILENT FILMS

TRIAL

VAUDEVILLE

VIRGINIA RAPPE

WILLIAM GOODRICH (Arbuckle's pseudonym in later life)

```
L M C V L X V N C O N K L I N G T F T
M A G I F N P Z T D P T H N K G U U C
M N R R J M J X X O Q J P R H I M N G
E S Q G K A B E X O N E R A T I O N W
A L I I M U R M O W C B F F Y K B T I
F A L N X D O Y T Y H T C Y D A U R L
E U P I M E T S F L A K Y F P X S U L
L G L A V D C G L L R Y E K X B T S I
K H A R T E A D V O L I O X G I E M A
C T I A V L D H S H I N P A Q A R L M
U E R P T M P U Z Y E Z R S E L K I G
B R T P P O X Y A J C S N X J G E F O
R E G E L N U I C V H O Y D U O A T O
A K R B T T H F S X A L J R C X T N D
S A F N Z L H G J O P R O S U H O E R
F A C Q U I T T A L L Y O F N M N L I
Z T N U O M A R A P I R U T O L W I C
E J L W F A N J H U N G J U R I E S H
V N A I D E M O C L P D O C B S V A R
```

Answers on page 176.

Cryptograms are messages in substitution code. Break the code to read the message. For example, THE SMART CAT might become FVO QWGDF JGF if **F** is substituted for **T**, **V** for **H**, **O** for **E**, and so on.

UYBBLN UDKGYLK CYLC YG 1573, ZPKGLC DO OSL NODAL. D SLKEYO, SL RDN DWWPNLC HM ZLYGU D RLKLRHBM—NILWYMYWDBBV, HM AYBBYGU DGC LDOYGU MHPK WSYBCKLG. SL BYQLC YG MKDGWL.

                                    Answers on page 176

COLD CASE

Change just one letter on each line to go from the top word to the bottom word. Do not change the order of the letters. You must have a common English word at each step.

COLD

_____

_____

_____

_____

_____

CASE

Answers on page 176.

The tiny island nation of Khafar has had a tumultuous history. Five of its kings have been poisoned in the past century alone, each by a different relative and with a different type of poison. Using only the clues below, determine the year in which each king died, who killed him, and the name of the poison that was used.

1. Of King Taton-on and whoever was poisoned with hemlock, one died in 1938 and the other was murdered by his uncle.

2. The arsenic poisoning occurred 17 years before King Kaponi's untimely end.

3. The king who was poisoned by his eldest son died 34 years before the one who died of oleander poisoning.

4. Of King Anjiwat and whoever was killed in 1921, one was poisoned by his wife and the other by hemlock.

5. King Lilamaku, who died sometime after 1910, wasn't murdered by either his cousin or his uncle.

6. King Anjiwat died of strychnine poisoning in 1972.

	Kings					Killers					Poisons				
	Anjiwat	Kaponi	Lilamaku	Taton-on	Veri'ma	Brother	Cousin	Son	Uncle	Wife	Arsenic	Cyanide	Hemlock	Oleander	Strychnine
Years 1904															
1921															
1938															
1955															
1972															
Poisons Arsenic															
Cyanide										
Hemlock										
Oleander										
Strychnine										
Killers Brother					
Cousin					
Son					
Uncle					
Wife					

Years	Kings	Killers	Poisons
1904			
1921			
1938			
1955			
1972			

Answers on page 176.

Read this true crime account, then turn to the next page to test your knowledge.

Following the rise of the National Crime Syndicate, or what people now call the Mafia, a group of enterprising killers formed an enforcement arm that the press dubbed "Murder, Incorporated." They were also known as "The Combination" or "The Brownsville Boys," since many of them came from Brooklyn's Brownsville area.

The Combination began their mayhem-for-money operation around 1930 following the formation of the National Crime Syndicate. Until their demise in the mid-1940s, they enforced the rules of organized crime through fear, intimidation, and murder. Most of the group's members were Jewish and Italian gangsters from Brooklyn; remorseless and bloodthirsty, murder for money was their stock-in-trade. The number of murders committed during their bloody reign is unknown even today, but estimates put the total at more than a thousand from coast to coast. The title "Murder, Incorporated" was the invention of a fearless *New York World-Telegram* police reporter named Harry Feeney; the name stuck.

The formation of the group was the brainchild of mob overlords Johnny Torrio and "Lucky" Luciano. The most high-profile assassination credited to the enterprise was the murder of gang lord Dutch Schultz, who defied the syndicate's orders to abandon a plan to assassinate New York crime-buster Thomas Dewey. The job went to one of the Combination's top-echelon gunsels, Charles "Charlie the Bug" Workman, whose bloody prowess ranked alongside such Murder, Inc., elite as Louis "Lepke" Buchalter, the man who issued the orders; Albert Anastasia, the lord high executioner; Abe "Kid Twist" Reles, whose eventual capitulation led to the group's downfall; Louis Capone (no relation to Al); Frank Abbandando; Harry "Pittsburg Phil" Strauss, an expert with an ice pick; Martin "Buggsy" Goldstein; Harry "Happy" Maione, leader of the Italian faction; Emanuel "Mendy" Weiss, who is rumored to have never committed murder on the Sabbath; Johnny Dio; Albert "Allie" Tannenbaum; Irving "Knadles" Nitzberg, who twice beat a death sentence when his convictions were overturned; Vito "Socko" Gurino; Jacob Drucker; Philip "Little Farvel" Cohen; and Sholom Bernstein, who like many of his cohorts turned against his mentors to save his own life. It was an era of infamy unequaled in mob lore.

Though many of the rank and file of Murder, Inc., appeared to enjoy killing, Reles, a former soda jerk, killed only as a matter of business. Known as "Kid Twist," Reles may not have been as bloodthirsty as some of his contemporaries, but he was cursed with a huge ego and a big mouth, and he wasn't shy about doing his bragging in front of cops, judges, the press, or the public at large. The little man with the big mouth would eventually lead to the unraveling of the Combination and greatly weaken the power of the National Crime Syndicate. When an informant fingered Reles and "Buggsy" Goldstein for the murder of a small-time hood, both men turned themselves in, believing they could beat the rap just as they had a dozen times before, but this one was ironclad. Reles sang loud and clear, implicating his peers and bosses in more than 80 murders and sending several of them to the electric chair, including the untouchable Buchalter. He also revealed the internal secret structure of the National Syndicate. Reles was in protective custody when he "fell" to his death from a hotel room on November 12, 1941, while surrounded by police. By the mid-1940s, Murder, Inc., was a thing of the past, and the National Crime Syndicate was in decline. When it came to singing like a canary, only Joe Valachi would surpass the performance of Reles, once the most trusted member of the Brownsville Boys.

(Do not read this until you have read the previous page!)

1. The name "Murder, Incorporated" came from this source.

    A. The police

    B. The Brownsville Boys themselves

    C. A member of the press

    D. Al Capone

2. The Combination are believed to be responsible for about this many deaths.

    A. 120

    B. 500

    C. 1,000

    D. 3,400

3. This member was an "expert with an ice pick."

    A. Louis Capone

    B. Harry Strauss

    C. Abe Reles

    D. Albert Anastasia

4. Reles was arrested along with this other man.

    A. "Buggsy" Goldstein

    B. Louis "Lepke" Buchalter

    C. "Lucky" Luciano

    D. Sholom Bernstein

Answers on page 177.

Study this picture of the crime scene for 1 minute, then turn the page.

Answers on page 177.

(Do not read this until you have read the previous page!) Which image exactly matches the crime scene?

1.

2.

3.

4.

FIND THE WITNESS

On Carbon Lane, there are 5 houses that are identical to each other. You need to follow up with a witness to a car accident on his street, Manuel Rodriguez, but without any address on the doors you are not sure which house to approach. You know that from a previous statement that Rodriguez lives with his wife and at least one daughter. The staff at the corner bar and your own observations give you some clues. From the information given, can you find the right house?

A. There are two houses where the only kids are boys. One is house A. The other is either house C or house D.

B. There is a widow who lives by herself somewhere on the block, who has said she loves what her next door neighbors do with their garden and how they get their daughters involved.

C. The couple without children has children living on either side of their house.

D. Mr. Rodriguez said at the initial interview that he didn't think that the neighbors on either side of him were home when the car accident happened, as they would have been at work or school.

House A   House B

House C

House D

House E

            Answers on page 177.

MOTEL HIDEOUT

A thief hides out in one of the 45 motel rooms listed in the chart below. The motel's in-house detective received a sheet of four clues, signed "The Logical Thief." Using these clues, the detective found the room number within 15 minutes—but by that time, the thief had fled. Can you find the thief's motel room quicker?

1. Multiply the first digit by 2 to get the second digit.
2. The first digit is a prime number.
3. The second digit is not prime.
4. It is not divisible by 9.

51	52	53	54	55	56	57	58	59
41	42	43	44	45	46	47	48	49
31	32	33	34	35	36	37	38	39
21	22	23	24	25	26	27	28	29
11	12	13	14	15	16	17	18	19

Answers on page 177.

Match each criminal's name at birth in the top list to a name or names by which he or she was later known in the bottom list.

NAME AT BIRTH

1. Herman Webster Mudgett (find 2)

2. Henry McCarty (find 2)

3. Myra Shirley

4. Charles Earl Bowles

5. Robert Leroy Parker

6. Harry Alonzo Longabaugh

7. Arizona Clark

LATER KNOWN AS

A. The Sundance Kid

B. Henry Howard

C. William Bonney

D. Belle Star

E. Kate "Ma" Barker

F. Black Bart

G. Butch Cassidy

H. Billy the Kid

I. H. H. Holmes

Answers on page 177.

Every word listed is contained within the group of letters. Words can be found in a straight line horizontally, vertically, or diagonally. They may be read either forward or backward.

ABBY (stepmother)

ALIBI

ANDREW (father)

AXE

BRIDGET (maid)

CONTRADICTIONS

EMMA (sister)

FALL RIVER

FATHER

FUGUE STATE THEORY

HATCHET

INQUEST

MURDER WEAPON

PRUSSIC ACID (recent purchase)

RUMORS

SHOPLIFTING

STEPMOTHER

SUSPECTED POISONING

TESTIMONY

TRIAL

```
T U A N D M E Z M J L R K S D S G P X
M B V E Y Y Y J P I E J N K I D F I R
P F X G Y F O X F H W O H S C E M M A
A A V A X D W M T N I G H F A P J S U
B L L H L B R O V T E O G N C B D B L
Q C G X G I M I C P P F T R I A L T T
J B Z X Z P B I I L X N M Y S B H S E
K V X G E P D I I Q O U M Q S R O E S
K V S T U A N F L P C X Q S U I F U T
H X S M R W T B A P E S E E R D O Q I
H U C T H I L E V F E R E N P G H N M
B A N Q N A W V A K P O X O G E M I O
F O T G W R Y V L W H M J X K T O L N
C Q F C E E E O K H E U P A P W J V Y
D B I D H C R F A L L R I V E R G B N
S Q R I O E U D T P M V A I Y N B F H
Z U P G L C T D N F A T H E R A K W J
M Y R O E H T E T A T S E U G U F M O
U S U S P E C T E D P O I S O N I N G
```

53

Change just one letter on each line to go from the top word to the bottom word. Do not change the order of the letters. You must have a common English word at each step.

LEAVE

_____

_____

_____

_____

_____

_____

_____

_____

_____

PRINT

Answers on page 177.

Read the story below, than turn the page and answer the questions.

The detective overheard the thief tell her accomplice about the different places where she stashed the loot. She said, "The ruby bracelet and the sapphire ring are both found in the summer house in Claremont Heights. The pearl necklace is hidden in the penthouse suite of the condo building in New York. The vintage wine is in the crawl-space of the farmhouse in Trevalyn. The gold coins are in the safety deposit box in the bank in Potosie."

(Do not read this until you have read the previous page!)

The investigator overheard the information about where the stolen loot was stored, but didn't have anywhere to write it down! Answer the questions below to help the investigator remember.

1. Two items are found at the summer house. What are they?

    A. Ruby bracelet and sapphire ring

    B. Ruby ring and sapphire bracelet

    C. Ruby bracelet and pearl necklace

    D. Ruby bracelet and gold coins

2. The pearl necklace is found in this location.

    A. Claremont Heights

    B. New York

    C. Trevalyn

    D. Potosie

3. The vintage wine is found in this part of the farmhouse.

    A. Attic

    B. Basement

    C. Crawlspace

    D. Safe

4. The bank is found in this location.

    A. Claremont Heights

    B. New York

    C. Trevalyn

    D. Potosie

Answers on page 178.

Cryptograms are messages in substitution code. Break the code to read the message. For example, THE SMART CAT might become FVO QWGDF JGF if **F** is substituted for **T**, **V** for **H**, **O** for **E**, and so on.

OGAN PAHHVL TKN BFLE AE NDFOHKEQ BRO CFSVQ
OF MKCKADK, TGVLV GV NVO RI KE VNOKOV DKHHVQ
VQAEBRLZG DKNOHV. OLKSVHVLN TGF KIILFKDGVQ
OGV DKNOHV OFF DHFNVHX OVEQVQ OF QANKIIVKL.
GV LVIFLOVQHX OFNNVQ GAN SADOACN AEOF K
NAEPGFHV. GV TKN DKHHVQ OGV CKQ CKNOVL FL OGV
CKQ QFDOFL FW VQAEBRLZG. GV VSVEORKHHX NGFO
K NFHQAVL TGF GKQ BVVE NVEO OF DKIORLV GAC. GV
OGVE OLAVQ OF WHVV OGV KLVK, BRO TKN DKRZGO,
OLAVQ, KEQ GKEZVQ.

Answers on page 178.

Read this true crime account, then turn to the next page to test your knowledge.

Bonnie and Clyde, Texas's most notorious outlaws, rose to fame during the Great Depression of the 1930s. The pair gained a mythical, Robin Hood–like status, but the real Bonnie and Clyde were very different from the figures portrayed by the popular media.

The early 1930s was a time when businesses folded at an unprecedented rate and plummeting crop prices forced farmers from their lands in record numbers. Men desperate for work trawled city streets looking for jobs, soup kitchens were swamped, and the value of a dollar plunged. When Bonnie and Clyde began their crime spree, the public viewed them as outsiders fighting back against an uncaring system that had failed the working man.

Bonnie Parker was born on October 1, 1910, in Rowena. When she met Clyde Barrow in 1930, she was already married to a man used to being on the wrong side of the law. However, Bonnie was not a typical gangster's moll. She was an honor-roll student in high school who excelled in creative writing and even won a spelling championship. After her husband was sentenced to the penitentiary, Bonnie scraped together a living by working as a waitress in West Dallas. Then Clyde Barrow entered her life.

Clyde was born on March 24, 1909, in Telico, just south of Dallas, and spent more of his poverty-stricken youth in trouble with the law than he did in school. He was arrested for stealing turkeys, auto theft, and safecracking. Soon after his romance with Bonnie began, he was sentenced to two years for a number of burglaries and car thefts. Bonnie managed to smuggle a Colt revolver to him, and Clyde was able to escape with his cell mate, William Turner.

Clyde and Turner were soon recaptured and sentenced to 14 years at the Texas State Penitentiary. But Clyde was pardoned in February 1932 after his mother intervened and Clyde had even had a fellow inmate chop off two of his toes in order to garner sympathy.

After two months of attempting to go straight, Clyde started a crime spree with Bonnie that stretched from Texas to Oklahoma, Missouri, Iowa, New Mexico, and Louisiana. They robbed gas stations, liquor stores, banks, and jewelry stores. They also captured the public imagination by frequently taking hostages as they made their daring escapes and then releasing them unharmed when they were out of danger. Other outlaws came and went from the Barrow Gang, but it was only after several of the robberies culminated in murder that public opinion turned against Bonnie and Clyde.

In total, the Barrow Gang is believed to have murdered at least nine police officers and several civilians during their robberies. While Bonnie posed alongside Clyde clutching a machine gun for photos, many argue that at no time did she ever fire a weapon, let alone kill or injure anyone. Another popular misconception had her dubbed as the cigar-smoking moll of the Barrow Gang. Again, Bonnie was known to smoke only cigarettes, but she once posed with a cigar in what became a famous photograph.

The end came on May 23, 1934, along a desolate road in Bienville Parish, Louisiana. The gang had murdered two Texas police officers, so Bonnie and Clyde were on the run again. A posse of four Texas Rangers and two Louisiana officers waited patiently for hours near the gang's hideout. When Bonnie and Clyde pulled up, the lawmen opened fire, pumping 167 rounds into the outlaws' car. So many gunshots hit the pair that the fingers on Bonnie's right hand were blown away. At the time of their deaths, Bonnie was 23 years old; Clyde, 24.

(Do not read this until you have read the previous page!)

1. Bonnie and Clyde came from this state but were eventually killed in this state.

  A. Texas, Louisiana

  B. Louisiana, Texas

  C. Texas, Ohio

  D. Texas, California

2. Clyde had a fellow inmate do this to drum up sympathy.

  A. Hit him

  B. Scar his face

  C. Cut off two toes

  D. Cut off two fingers

3. Bonnie and Clyde's gang never murdered anyone during their robberies.

  _____ True

  _____ False

4. Clyde had been arrested for the crime of safecracking before he met Bonnie.

  _____ True

  _____ False

Answers on page 178.

Study this picture of the crime scene for 1 minute, then turn the page.

(Do not read this until you have read the previous page!) Which image exactly matches the crime scene?

1.

2.

3.

4.

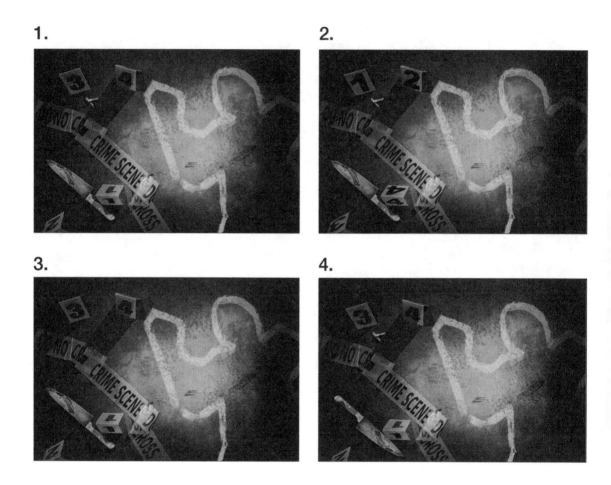

Answers on page 178.

MOTEL HIDEOUT

A thief hides out in one of the 45 motel rooms listed in the chart below. The motel's in-house detective received a sheet of four clues, signed "The Logical Thief." Using these clues, the detective found the room number within 15 minutes—but by that time, the thief had fled. Can you find the thief's motel room quicker?

1. Both digits are odd.

2. The first digit is equal to or greater than the second digit.

3. The sum of the digits is 5 or less.

4. The first digit is not divisible by 3.

51	52	53	54	55	56	57	58	59
41	42	43	44	45	46	47	48	49
31	32	33	34	35	36	37	38	39
21	22	23	24	25	26	27	28	29
11	12	13	14	15	16	17	18	19

Answers on page 178.

Every word listed is contained within the group of letters. Words can be found in a straight line horizontally, vertically, or diagonally. They may be read either forward or backward.

BOEING

BOMB THREAT

BRIEFCASE

COCKPIT

FLIGHT

HIJACKER

PARACHUTE

PORTLAND

RANSOM

RIP CORD

RIVERBANK

SEARCH OPERATIONS

SERIAL NUMBERS

THANKSGIVING EVE

TIE CLIP

UNMARKED BILLS

UNSOLVED

WASHINGTON

```
Y  F  H  Z  E  F  W  D  I  X  L  G  Q  E  M  S  Y  J  U
P  A  P  B  K  S  E  L  X  Z  Q  F  Q  P  H  N  J  S  J
O  R  F  L  R  V  A  S  V  W  M  L  G  X  Q  O  I  M  Y
J  O  X  I  L  E  R  C  C  M  X  I  N  Y  H  I  C  K  E
C  W  S  O  H  J  K  M  F  U  Y  G  H  H  P  T  I  Q  E
S  S  S  A  S  D  Z  C  X  E  C  H  F  L  P  A  K  L  H
O  N  E  H  L  W  O  R  A  K  I  T  Z  A  H  R  F  Q  T
U  P  P  R  L  I  J  H  N  J  Z  R  R  K  W  E  L  T  C
V  I  T  B  I  M  X  A  R  C  I  A  B  A  D  P  X  I  L
W  L  L  E  B  A  B  X  D  A  C  H  S  K  V  O  R  P  B
N  C  X  G  D  R  L  Q  A  V  N  H  L  D  A  H  I  K  O
P  E  I  V  E  Q  W  N  U  G  I  S  H  A  Y  C  P  C  M
O  I  F  V  K  O  A  T  U  N  C  G  O  M  G  R  C  O  B
R  T  I  V  R  V  E  Y  G  M  V  P  C  M  L  A  O  C  T
T  R  K  R  A  B  R  T  K  Y  B  I  S  G  N  E  R  J  H
L  C  P  E  M  Y  O  V  R  B  O  E  I  N  G  S  D  F  R
A  Z  K  E  N  N  Y  H  N  Q  X  F  R  H  I  C  F  A  E
N  J  W  U  U  S  G  P  G  Z  E  K  I  S  D  W  T  U  A
D  T  H  A  N  K  S  G  I  V  I  N  G  E  V  E  L  X  T
```

Answers on page 179.

Read this true crime account, then turn to the next page to test your knowledge.

There's no disputing that dictionaries are valuable tools. But did you ever stop to wonder who originally compiled the words in these syllabic storehouses? Certainly, anyone vying to be the authoritative word on, well, words, would need credentials above reproach. Right?

Wrong. The decidedly highbrow *Oxford English Dictionary (OED)*—the reference book of note that many turn to when they wish to mimic the King's English—was created in part by a murderer. In fact, this murderer was one of the book's most prolific contributors. Who knew?

Inititally called the *New English Dictionary (NED),* the compendium was a project initiated by the Philological Society of London in 1857. It was a daunting task by any yardstick. From 1879 (the year real work on the *NED* began) until its 1928 completion, tens of thousands of definitions would be culled from a small army of donors. One of these contributors was Dr. William Chester Minor, a retired American surgeon who had served the Union Army during the Civil War. During his military stint, the surgeon would witness horrible atrocities at the famed Battle of the Wilderness. This experience, along with other horrifying wartime encounters, would inflict emotional scars that would eventually drive the doctor completely over the brink.

Answering an ad seeking literary contributions, Minor first came to the attention of Professor James Murray, the *NED*'s chief editor from 1879 until his death in 1915. Impressed by the neat, well-researched quotes that Minor had mailed to him, Murray accepted the material for inclusion in the dictionary. As a sensationalized account of the story goes, after a few such go-rounds, Professor Murray asked the man to meet him in Oxford so they could discuss future work. Each time the editor made the gesture, he was politely rebuffed. This baffled Murray. He knew that Minor was located just 50 miles away at the Broadmoor Criminal Lunatic Asylum and had assumed that he was one of their doctors. Surely the physician could take a brief leave from his duties to discuss the Dictionary in person?

But Minor wasn't part of Broadmoor's staff. He was a patient whose grip on reality was tenuous at best. Minor killed a laborer whom he thought meant him harm and was consequently judged insane and permanently confined to the asylum.

Eventually, Minor relented and allowed Murray to meet him at the facility. One can only imagine the editor's shock when he arrived to discover that his prized contributor was a homicidal madman. After allowing the truth to gel, Murray was undeterred. It was obvious that Minor, despite his demons, was meticulous in his research and gifted in his application. It was also obvious that he could use a friend.

Murray would continue to accept Minor's dictionary contributions and visit him regularly until 1910, the year the troubled man was relocated to the United States. In the end, Minor was one of the most prolific contributors to the *NED.* Why had Murray been so keen to accept contributions from a stark, raving madman? As any seasoned editor will tell you, ability is where you find it—and when you find it, you hang on tight. Minor had the stuff, and Murray knew it. And, as it now happens, so do you.

FINDING MURDER IN THE DICTIONARY (PART II)

(Do not read this until you have read the previous page!)

1. Dr. Minor was an army surgeon in this war.

    A. Boer War

    B. World War I

    C. U.S. Civil War

    D. Crimean War

2. Minor lived at this institution.

    A. Broadmoor Criminal Lunatic Asylum

    B. Broadbent Criminal Lunatic Asylum

    C. Oxford Asylum for the Insane

    D. Murray Institution for the Criminally Insane

3. The OED was previously called this.

    A. New English Dictionary (NED)

    B. London English Dictionary (LED)

    C. Necessary English Dictionary (NED)

    D. It was always known as the Oxford English Dictionary (OED)

4. Minor was institutionalized for the murder of:

    A. One person

    B. Three people

    C. A killing spree of twenty people

    D. An unknown number of persons

Answers on page 179.

Study this picture of the crime scene for 1 minute, then turn the page.

(Do not read this until you have read the previous page!)

1. The laptop was right side up.

_____ True

_____ False

2. A sheet of paper was found on top of the briefcase.

_____ True

_____ False

3. A smartphone was found to the left of the laptop.

_____ True

_____ False

4. The investigator was wearing booties over his regular footware.

_____ True

_____ False

Answers on page 179

MOTEL HIDEOUT

A thief hides out in one of the 45 motel rooms listed in the chart below. The motel's in-house detective received a sheet of four clues, signed "The Logical Thief." Using these clues, the detective found the room number within 15 minutes—but by that time, the thief had fled. Can you find the thief's motel room quicker?

1. The number is divisible by 4.

2. The second digit is larger than the first.

3. The second digit is divisible by 4.

4. The first digit is not a prime number.

51	52	53	54	55	56	57	58	59
41	42	43	44	45	46	47	48	49
31	32	33	34	35	36	37	38	39
21	22	23	24	25	26	27	28	29
11	12	13	14	15	16	17	18	19

71

Answers on page 179.

Susan works as a parking enforcement officer in downtown Charlotte. Today she wrote tickets for five illegally-parked cars. Help her sort out her paperwork by matching each ticket to the correct car (model and color), street location, and the time at which it was written.

1. The Toyota was ticketed one hour after the green car.

2. Of the Toyota and the Chevrolet, one was silver and the other was the last to be ticketed.

3. The ticket on Tawny Terrace was written at 12:00pm. Susan wrote the ticket for the silver car sometime before that.

4. The brown car was ticketed 2 hours after the Nissan.

5. Susan wrote the ticket on Sandy Street sometime before the one for the double-parked Chevrolet.

6. The Mazda was ticketed 2 hours after the black car.

7. Susan was on Apple Avenue sometime before 12:30pm.

8. The ticket on Lantern Lane wasn't written at 1:00pm.

	Models					Colors					Locations				
	Chevrolet	Honda	Nissan	Mazda	Toyota	Black	Blue	Brown	Green	Silver	Apple Ave.	Lantern Ln.	Raffle Rd.	Sandy St.	Tawny Terr.
Times 10:00am															
11:00am															
12:00pm															
1:00pm															
2:00pm															
Locations Apple Ave.															
Lantern Ln.															
Raffle Rd.															
Sandy St.															
Tawny Terr.															
Colors Black															
Blue															
Brown															
Green															
Silver															

Times	Models	Colors	Locations
10:00am			
11:00am			
12:00pm			
1:00pm			
2:00pm			

73

Answers on page 179.

Every word listed is contained within the group of letters. Words can be found in a straight line horizontally, vertically, or diagonally. They may be read either forward or backward.

CANONICAL FIVE

"DEAR BOSS" (letter)

"FROM HELL" (letter)

LEATHER APRON

LONDON

METROPOLITAN POLICE SERVICE

MUTILATION

ORGAN REMOVAL

PROSTITUTES

RIPPEROLOGY

"SAUCY JACKY" (postcard)

SERIAL KILLER

SCOTLAND YARD

THOMAS OPENSHAW

THROAT

VICTORIAN ERA

VIGILANCE COMMITTEE

WHITECHAPEL

```
C L H E A S T T D A L B V P R O S T I T U T E S M
E C I V R E S E C I L O P N A T I L O P O R T E M
Y B O P N D A K E N N L K C S A U C Y J A C K Y A
O Q L H J R C S N W Y B H K O S V C O B F G X L Q
C L P J B B F D Y Y W E H V U C J E Q V D N P D K
V W L O V H M R I G U N T T G O V D Z E D N N H R
R G S E M Y R R S I U X N C N I W T E N L T P T H
D S A X H U J M M J L H X S F V O D K Y Y D A D Y
R N S Y U M T N R D G N X L M J Q B K G V B E H T
A M P C R U O I E Q O X A W H Z D N O L Q Y J T H
Y J C V T L S R L T S C S J F E Q L J A V P I K O
D E M Q X S F E F A I P A G I H O T T V R W Q W M
N Q O M I H N T R N T F P P D R Y T X O R C H N A
A H M X R A Q V O I L I V J E H T W Z M Z P R O S
L N U W A Y R N H F A N O P X Q F M H E C R G R O
T T M X T V A L B O N L P N M D K Y Z R C F I P P
O I G T F C K M F Y S I K S V J F S J N N U Z A E
C Y X C N I N J Q N R C P I B U V V F A F W Y R N
S E E T T I M M O C E C N A L I G I V G B W N E S
C I K T Z H M J D E B A B F R L L P L R P V M H H
U R A O H T R W G C A P Z G O P E J O O Q K A T A
E G X S P R P P M E C R V I C T O R I A N E R A W
B D W V I G O J I Z S O E T V R L P L W C D O E V
W H I T E C H A P E L Y H X J Y F X U N Q P O L E
H M E B S Q O X T M A H E Q J I X C N L Y I A N P
```

75

MOTEL HIDEOUT

A thief hides out in one of the 45 motel rooms listed in the chart below. The motel's in-house detective received a sheet of four clues, signed "The Logical Thief." Using these clues, the detective found the room number within 15 minutes—but by that time, the thief had fled. Can you find the thief's motel room quicker?

1. Both digits are odd.

2. The second digit is divisible by 3.

3. The first digit is not divisible by 3 or 5.

4. The second digit is not a prime number.

51	52	53	54	55	56	57	58	59
41	42	43	44	45	46	47	48	49
31	32	33	34	35	36	37	38	39
21	22	23	24	25	26	27	28	29
11	12	13	14	15	16	17	18	19

76

Answers on page 180.

Read the story below, than turn the page and answer the questions.

The detective overheard the thief tell her accomplice about the different places where she stashed the loot. She said, "I left the largest diamond taped to the drainpipe underneath the upstairs sink. The four smaller diamonds are tucked in a pair of pantyhose in the third drawer down in the dresser. The gold necklace is wrapped up in the rose-patterned pillowcase in the linen closet. The gold bars are in a locked trunk in the attic."

(Do not read this until you have read the previous page!)

The investigator overheard the information about where the stolen loot was stored, but didn't have anywhere to write it down! Answer the questions below to help the investigator remember.

1. What is found in the drainpipe?

   A. The largest diamond

   B. The four smaller diamonds

   C. The gold necklace

   D. The pearl

2. The gold necklace is wrapped in this.

   A. Pantyhose

   B. Plain pillowcase

   C. Rose-patterned pillowcase

   D. Sock

3. The gold bars are in this.

   A. The linen closet

   B. A locked trunk in the attic

   C. A trunk in the crawlspace

   D. A trunk in the basement

4. Which item or items are found in the top dresser drawer?

   A. The largest diamond

   B. The four smaller diamonds

   C. The gold necklace

   D. None of them

Answers on page 180.

Cryptograms are messages in substitution code. Break the code to read the message. For example, THE SMART CAT might become FVO QWGDF JGF if **F** is substituted for **T, V** for **H, O** for **E,** and so on.

V. V. VXNQJF CYJC ZJOXDJ VJ HIDTJC 35. YT VYF
DJNSHYLJNU FVXDH NYOJ, VJ GXQQYHHJC S
TIQZJD XO QIDCJDF, HVXIPV HVJ JRSGH TIQZJD YF
ITKTXMT. YH QSU VSLJ ZJJT OJMJD HVST 10, ZIH YH
QSU VSLJ TIQZJDJC QXDJ HVST 100. VXNQJF MSF
SNFX S ZYPSQYFH, QSDDUYTP HVDJJ CYOOJDJTH
MXQJT. VXNQJF MSF SGHYLJ SH HVJ HYQJ XO HVJ
1893 MXDNC'F OSYD YT GVYGSPX, YNNYTXYF. VJ XMTJC
S ZIYNCYTP HX MVYGV VJ NIDJC LYGHYQF ITCJD HVJ
PIYCJ HVSH YH MSF S VXHJN; YH MSF NSHJD CIZZJC
HVJ QIDCJD VXHJN STC HVJ QIDCJD GSFHNJ OXD HVJ
KYNNYTPF VJ GXQQYHHJC HVJDJ.

          Answers on page 180.

Read this true crime account, then turn to the next page to test your knowledge.

John Wilkes Booth is well known for his assassination of President Abraham Lincoln at Ford's Theatre on April 14, 1865, but the rather lengthy list of his coconspirators has not been quite so memorable.

A popular Shakespearean stage actor who traveled the country performing, John Wilkes Booth could have kept busy enjoying his notoriety and fame. Instead, inspired by the secession of the Southern states that set off the Civil War, he was firmly entrenched in his racist beliefs and loyalty to the Confederacy. Once Lincoln freed the slaves in the rebelling states, a conviction took hold in Booth's mind branding the abolitionist president his archenemy. Dead set on bringing down Lincoln and preserving the Confederacy and the institution of slavery, Booth began to plot his attack. Initially, he planned to kidnap Lincoln and then ransom him for captive Confederate soldiers, but the conspiracy evolved, of course, into the first presidential assassination in U.S. history.

Booth, who was charismatic and persuasive, had no trouble forming a gang of like-minded conspirators. Samuel Arnold, George Atzerodt, David Herold, Lewis Powell, John Surratt, and Michael O'Laughlen all joined with Booth to design various plots that would achieve victory for the South and cause trouble for Lincoln and his backers.

Meeting regularly at a boardinghouse run by Mary Surratt, the mother of one of the conspirators, the club decided to kidnap Lincoln in early 1865. They would simply snatch him from his box at a play and then ransom him for a few imprisoned Confederate soldiers. It would be a twofold victory, as they would cause grievance for their nemesis and bring the Confederacy closer to victory. Their plan was thwarted, though, when Lincoln failed to appear at the scheduled event. Similar plans were hatched, but for various reasons, none of the kidnapping plots came to fruition. Frustrated with his inability to capture Lincoln and spurred by Lincoln's continued attempts to dismantle the system of slavery, Booth determined that kidnapping was simply not enough: Lincoln must die.

Arnold, John Surratt, and O'Laughlen later swore that they knew nothing of the plot to commit murder, but Atzerodt, Herold, and Powell most certainly did. They each had their own assigned roles in the grand assassination plot, unsuccessful though they were in carrying out those parts. Atzerodt was slated to assassinate Vice

President Andrew Johnson, while Powell and Herold were scheduled to kill Secretary of State William Seward. All three assassinations were planned for the same time on the evening of April 14.

Only Booth found complete success in the mission, however. Atzerodt apparently backed down from his assignment in fear. Powell cut a path of carnage through the Seward mansion, stabbing the secretary of state in the face and neck and wounding two of Seward's sons, a daughter, a soldier guarding Seward, and a messenger, although no one was killed. Herold had been with Powell but ran away when the mission didn't seem to be going smoothly. Booth shot Lincoln in the back of the head. The president died on the morning of April 15.

Booth immediately fled the scene, injuring a leg in his mad dash. He met up with Herold, and the pair was on the run for two weeks before finally being discovered on a small farm. The fugitives were holed up in a barn—Herold surrendered, but when Booth refused to do the same, soldiers set the barn on fire. In the ensuing melee, Booth was shot in the neck; he died a few hours later. Atzerodt, Herold, and Powell were hanged for their crimes, as was one more purported coconspirator, Mary Surratt. She ran the boardinghouse in which much of this plot was hatched, a plot that definitely included her son at various times. Her specific involvement and knowledge of the affair, however, has frequently been challenged.

The rest of the original coconspirators, as well as others with suspicious acquaintance to the group, were sentenced to jail time for their involvement.

(Do not read this until you have read the previous page!)

1. How many co-conspirators did Booth have?

    A. 2

    B. 3

    C. 4

    D. At least 6

2. Atzerodt's mission was this.

    A. To arrange Booth's getaway and escape.

    B. To kill Vice President Johnson

    C. To kidnap Vice President Johnson

    D. To kill Secretary of State Seward

3. Powell was caught before entering Seward's house.

    _____True

    _____ False

4. Mary Surratt was charged as a co-conspirator and hanged.

    _____True

    _____ False

          Answers on page 181.

On Calendar Court, there are 5 houses that are identical to each other. You need to follow up with a witness, Yvette White, but without any address on the doors you are not sure which house to approach. You know that from a previous statement that White and her husband have two children, a boy and a girl. The staff at the corner coffee shop and your own observations give you some clues. From the information given, can you find the right house?

A. One staff member says she knows that the couple in house A do not have children, but every other house has at least one child.

B. Another staff member isn't sure where White lives, but he says he's heard her say that she's lucky that both her next door neighbors have kids for her kids to play with.

C. There's a house with a newborn baby somewhere on the block, but not next door to White.

D. The house with the newborn is not next to the couple without children.

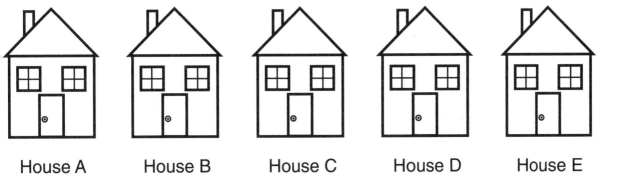

House A   House B   House C   House D   House E

Answers on page 181

THE "MOST HATED MAN IN THE WORLD"

In 1932, the kidnapping of Charles Lindbergh, Jr., son of the famous aviator and his wife Anne, shocked the nation. Although a ransom was paid, the child was murdered. Bruno Richard Hauptmann was accused and convicted of the crime. Every word listed is contained within the group of letters. Words can be found in a straight line horizontally, vertically, or diagonally. They may be read either forward or backward.

ABDUCTION

ANNE MORROW

CARPENTER

CHARLES

CRIME OF THE CENTURY

GOLD CERTIFICATE

ELECTRIC CHAIR

EXECUTION

JOHN CONDON

KIDNAPPING

LADDER

LINDBERGH

RANSOM NOTE

RICHARD HAUPTMANN

```
E C G Y Q J P J G N I E B N E R D
S R J K H Q V R S H V R R N T E Y
D I U I D N X K X K O A C A A D K
Y M X J F G M F I W N E M C D K
R E T N E P R A C S A O K T I A E
G O T Z G U H U O B D D D P F L L
N F I S N R U M D N E N A U I J E
I T G E X E N U I K J O N A T C C
P H Q X Z O C Y N M A C N H R X T
P E P K T T H B O J Q N E D E B R
A C J E I C A H I V X H M R C M I
N E T O X Y R V T B H O O A D O C
D N N R V E L W U H J J R H L K C
I T L I H R E D C Z R J R C O G H
K U V J U V S A E Q Q O O I G F A
N R M N U N B U X W H Y W R M T I
T Y C A R H G R E B D N I L X Z R
```

85   Answers on page 181.

Read this true crime account, then turn to the next page to test your knowledge.

The serial killer known as Jack the Ripper is one of history's most famous murderers. He breathed terror into the gas-lit streets and foggy back alleys of the Whitechapel area of London and became renowned the world over. Despite the countless books and movies detailing his story, however, his identity and motives remain shrouded in mystery. One of the most popular theories, espoused by the 2001 movie *From Hell* (starring Johnny Depp), links the killer to the British royal family.

Five murders are definitively attributed to Jack the Ripper, and he has variously been connected to at least six other unsolved slayings in the London area. The body of the first victim, 43-year-old Mary Ann Nichols, was discovered on the morning of August 31, 1888. Nichols's throat had been cut and her abdomen mutilated. The subsequent murders, which took place over a three-year period, grew in brutality. The killer removed the uterus of his second victim, Annie Chapman; part of the womb and left kidney of Catherine Eddowes; and the heart of Mary Kelly. All of his victims were prostitutes.

A man claiming to be the murderer sent a letter (dated September 25, 1888) to the Central News Agency, which passed it on to the Metropolitan Police. The letter included the line, "I am down on whores and I shant quit ripping them till I do get buckled." It was signed, "Yours truly, Jack the Ripper." A later postcard included the same sign-off. When police went public with details of the letters, the name "Jack the Ripper" stuck.

Officers from the Metropolitan Police and Scotland Yard had four main suspects: a poor Polish resident of Whitechapel by the name of Kosminski, a barrister who committed suicide in December 1888, a Russian-born thief, and an American doctor who fled to the States in November 1888 while on bail for gross indecency. Since there was little or no evidence against any of these men, the case spawned many conspiracy theories, the most popular of which links the killings to the royal family.

The heir to the British throne was Prince Albert Victor, grandson of Queen Victoria and son of the man who would later become King Edward VII. The prince, popularly known as Eddy, had a penchant for hanging around in the East End, and rumors abounded that he had a daughter, Alice, out of wedlock with a shop girl named Annie Crook. To prevent major embarrassment to the Crown, Eddy sought assistance from Queen Victoria's physician, Dr. William Gull, who institutionalized Annie to keep her quiet. However, her friends, including Mary Kelly, also knew the identity of Alice's father, so Dr. Gull created the persona of Jack the Ripper and brutally silenced them one by one. A variation on this theory has Dr. Gull acting without the knowledge of the prince, instead driven by madness resulting from a stroke he suffered in 1887.

Royal involvement would certainly explain why the police were unable to uncover the identity of the Ripper or to even settle on a prime suspect. There *was* a shop girl named Annie Crook who had an illegitimate daughter named Alice, but there is nothing to connect her to either the prince or the murdered prostitutes. In fact, there is no evidence to suggest that the murdered women knew one another. Until the identity of Jack the Ripper is settled beyond doubt, these and other conspiracy theories will likely persist.

(Do not read this until you have read the previous page!)

1. Jack the Ripper's first victim was:
   A. Mary Ann Nichols
   B. Annie Chapman
   C. Catherine Eddowes
   D. Mary Kelly

2. Prince Albert Victor was related to Queen Victoria in this way.
   A. Son
   B. Grandson
   C. Nephew
   D. Cousin

3. How many murders are definitively attributed to Jack the Ripper?
   A. Three
   B. Four
   C. Five
   D. Eleven

4. Who was Alice?
   A. One of Jack the Ripper's victims
   B. The prince's reported mistress
   C. The prince's reported child
   D. A witness

     Answers on page 181.

Study this picture of the crime scene for 1 minute, then turn the page.

(Do not read this until you have read the previous page!)

What changed between the image on the previous page and this one?

Answer on page 182.

Read the story below, than turn the page and answer the questions.

The detective overheard the jewelry thief tell his accomplice about the different places where he stashed the loot. He said, "The pearls are inside the egg carton in the fridge. The opals are in the ice cube tray in the freezer. The rubies are in the cereal box. The garnets are in the medicine cabinet in the upstairs bathroom."

(Do not read this until you have read the previous page!)

The investigator overheard the information about where the stolen loot was stored, but didn't have anywhere to write it down! Answer the questions below to help the investigator remember.

1. The garnets are found in this room.
    A. Kitchen
    B. Upstairs bathroom
    C. Downstairs bathroom
    D. We are not told.

2. The pearls are found in this location.
    A. Refrigerator
    B. Freezer
    C. Kitchen cabinet
    D. Medicine cabinet

3. What is found in the ice cube tray?
    A. Pearls
    B. Opals
    C. Rubies
    D. Garnets

4. What is found in the cereal box?
    A. Pearls
    B. Opals
    C. Rubies
    D. Garnets

                                      Answers on page 182.

Cryptograms are messages in substitution code. Break the code to read the message. For example, THE SMART CAT might become FVO QWGDF JGF if **F** is substituted for **T**, **V** for **H**, **O** for **E**, and so on.

RIP IWMKP NMJRIPMO FAVWBWI WHG UAEPY EATPG AH RIP EWRP 1700O. FAVWBWI UWO VWEEPG RIP "NAC IWMKP" WHG IAO NMJRIPM RIP "EARREP IWMKP." RIPY UPMP IACIUWYFWH WHG "MATPM KAMWRPO," FPH UIJ KMPYPG JH OIAKO. FAVWBWI UWO DAEEPG NY W TPHCPQSE KJOOP AH 1799, UIAEP UAEPY FWHWCPG RJ PTWGP BSORAVP SHRAE IP UWO VWSCIR, RMAPG, WHG PXPVSRPG AH 1804. WR RIP RAFP, IP UWO RMYAHC RJ VJEEPVR W MPUWMG NY RSMHAHC AH RIP IPWG JQ W QPEEJU VMAFAHWE.

Answers on page 182.

Read this true crime account, then turn to the next page to test your knowledge.

In an era known for its long list of public enemies, John Dillinger and his crew stood out more like endeared celebrities than the convicted killers and robbers they were known to be. The public, demoralized by the ongoing Depression, lacked financial and bureaucratic faith after suffering devastating losses at what they saw to be the hands of irresponsible government and financial institutions. When Dillinger and his charismatic crew began tearing through banks, they not only provided an exciting and dramatic media distraction, they also destroyed banks' potentially devastating mortgage paperwork in their wake. The masses seemed eager to clasp onto the real-life drama and connect it to their own plight.

Law officials weren't so keen on the criminals. J. Edgar Hoover and his newly formed Federal Bureau of Investigation were weary of gangsters' soft public perception and crafted a series of hard-hitting laws meant to immobilize them. Dillinger, one of the most prominent, popular, and evasive of the lot, was at the top of Hoover's hit list.

Dillinger had fled the supposedly escape-proof county jail in Crown Point, Indiana, in March 1934. A month and a few bank robberies later, Dillinger and company ended up hiding out in a woodsy Wisconsin lodge called Little Bohemia. Tipped off by the lodge owner's wife, Hoover and a team of federal investigators from Chicago responded with an ill-fated ambush that would go down in history as one of the greatest federal fiascoes of all time.

The Dillinger gang, including well-known characters such as Harry Pierpont and "Baby Face" Nelson, plus gang members' wives and girlfriends, had planned only a short layover at the wilderness retreat. Although owner Emil Wanatka and wife Nan had befriended an outlaw or two during the days of Prohibition, the Dillinger crew was a notch or two above the types they had known. So, upon discovering that their new slew of guests were members of the notorious gang, Wanatka made a bold move and confronted them. Dillinger assured him that they would be of no inconvenience and would not stay long.

However, Wanatka and his wife were basically held hostage at their humble hostel for the entire length of the Dillinger gang's stay. Telephone calls were monitored, lodge visitors were subject to scrutiny at both arrival and departure, and anyone who went into town for supplies was forced to travel with a Dillinger escort.

Knowing that any lodge departure would be surveyed closely, the Wanatkas decided to plant a note on Nan to pass to police. They would convince the gangsters that she and their ten-year-old son were merely departing for a nephew's birthday party and then would find a way to transmit their cry for help. Although Dillinger gave permission for the pair's trip, the frightened mother soon discovered "Baby Face" Nelson hot on their trail and ready to jump at the first sight of suspicious activity. Still, Nan managed to pass word to her family, who then contacted the authorities. Officials planned a siege. Unfortunately, Dillinger and company were not easily taken. As FBI agents Hugh Clegg and Melvin Purvis approached, the lodge's watchdogs barked at the strangers—though only after a series of miscalculated gunshots did the Dillinger gang stir. The agents had mistakenly fired at three patrons leaving the lodge's bar, killing one and wounding the others. The Dillinger gang knew their hideout had been discovered.

The ever-elusive bunch had plotted an escape plan upon their arrival. The agents didn't have the same knowledge of the land's lay and fell victim to a nearby ditch and a wall of barbed wire. Wounded and entangled, the agents were sitting ducks. Their suspects were free to flee and take their turn at gunfire.

Hoover had pledged a significant story to the press in anticipation of the planned attack. Unluckily for him, the story would be a hellish one. The ambush resulted in not a single loss for the Dillinger gang. On the other side were two injured law officers, two wounded bystanders, and the death of a complete innocent.

Although Purvis didn't find success on that infamous day, he would eventually have another chance. On July 22, 1934, Dillinger was shot dead by Purvis's agents outside a Chicago cinema.

(Do not read this until you have read the previous page!)

1. The incident at Little Bohemia took place in this year.

    A. 1929

    B. 1931

    C. 1933

    D. 1934

2. Nan passed along the message about the Dillinger's on this occasion.

    A. Her nephew's birthday party

    B. Her son's birthday party

    C. Her sister's birthday party

    D. A family wedding

3. Little Bohemia was . . .

    A. The name of the town

    B. The nickname for that part of Wisconsin

    C. The name of the lodge

    D. The name of the nearest city

4. Dillinger was killed the same year as the shootout.

    _____ True

    _____ False

Answers on page 182.

MOTEL HIDEOUT

A thief hides out in one of the 45 motel rooms listed in the chart below. The motel's in-house detective received a sheet of four clues, signed "The Logical Thief." Using these clues, the detective found the room number within 15 minutes—but by that time, the thief had fled. Can you find the thief's motel room quicker?

1. The first digit is a prime number.

2. Both digits are even.

3. The second digit cannot be divided by 3.

4. The second digit is not larger than the first digit.

51	52	53	54	55	56	57	58	59
41	42	43	44	45	46	47	48	49
31	32	33	34	35	36	37	38	39
21	22	23	24	25	26	27	28	29
11	12	13	14	15	16	17	18	19

Answers on page 183.

Every word listed is contained within the group of letters. Words can be found in a straight line horizontally, vertically, or diagonally. They may be read either forward or backward.

ANULA (This ancient queen regnant poisoned four husbands around 50 BC.)

CATHERINE MONVOISIN (Monvoison was burned at the stake in 1620, accused of poisonings and the ritual murder of more than 1,000 people.)

CHRISTMAN GENIPPERTEINGA (This German bandit from the 1500s reportedly killed over 950 people, and was trying for 1,000.)

ELIZABETH BATHORY (This Hungarian noblewoman tortured and killed hundreds of girls, earning herself the name "The Blood Countess.")

GILLES DE RAIS (This French nobleman who lived ~1405–1440 is believed to have claimed more than 140 child victims.)

JASPER HANEBUTH (This highwayman from the 1600s was active in Eilinriede Forest.)

LEWIS HUTCHINSON (This Scot from the 1700s was known as "The Mad Doctor of Edinburgh Castle.")

LOCUSTA OF GAUL (She made poisons for Nero around 55 AD, but was executed by his successor.)

PETER STUMMP (Called "The Werewolf of Bedburg," he was accused of cannibalism and witchcraft.)

THUG BEHRAM (This leader of the Thuggee group of robbers and murderers lived in India in the early 1800s.)

```
A R P Z E L I Z A B E T H B A T H O R Y H W E
G W Q J O B W N H Z B L I H E M S C U H H A E
N O L I Q A N J P M B Z S Q G A T X Y L X S N
I U W X N L U A Q M P O H V L U O S L U K N I
E U T Y E Q K S W A E W Y U J K I U Q A N L S
T E I S H J W P G J J G N Y O K N G Q G A G I
R L W R Q X L E I U S A R K B K O P O F I C O
E A J P T A T R L Y Q U K U T I S F H O Q H V
P P N H A T R H L E A K T A C K N V C A K V N
P O X U K I G A E F Y X P T F D I P Z T O U O
I T E A Z M G N S E Q C M C D T H C R S P D M
N B B Q F Y Z E D V N C M L R C C O C U H J E
E G P K K U A B E W F L U I U V T T N C W E N
G W U C T D S U R D C K T U M Q U L F O F K I
N Q D B G L G T A P D J S A Y I H I P L W A R
A G H Z C I W H I J I G R M P L S C F F G Q E
M L V M J V P E S K E H E M L B I R B C U G H
T S H F P A W L P E E A T G C Q W Q R A A Z T
S C I L C O R T Z B M L E K G G E H O Y D C A
I O J P E N X K G Q C M P C C O L E O B O R C
R T Y E X G X U P O N C K A G U K B V Z P H A
H X V I I V H S W I H P K R W Y E D W U R D V
C H V I I T C C S R I G S V K K U W Y H U M I
```

Answers on page 183.

LOST LIBRARY BOOKS

Middleworth Library considers books that have been overdue for more than 6 months to be officially "lost" and sends a library detective out to try to retrieve them from the last person to have borrowed them. This week five such books have been reported as lost. Help the library detective find them by matching each book to its author and publication date, and determine the name of the last person to have borrowed each book from the library.

1. Midge Mintz didn't publish any books in the 1940s.

2. *In or Out,* the book Edith borrowed, and the one published in 1970 are three different books.

3. Heddy Heath's book came out 13 years after Keith Koch's.

4. The book last borrowed by Danica was either *Grey Skies* or the one written by Midge Mintz.

5. *High Tide* was published 26 years after *Just Friends.*

6. Of Nick Norris's book and *High Tide,* one was borrowed by Charles and the other by Bailey.

7. Keith Koch's book came out 13 years before *In or Out.*

8. The book Bailey borrowed was published 26 years after the one Angelica took out.

9. Charles borrowed a book that was published in 1970.

	Borrowers					Authors					Titles				
	Angelica	Bailey	Charles	Danica	Edith	Heddy Heath	Jim Joyner	Keith Koch	Midge Mintz	Nick Norris	Fine Days	Grey Skies	High Tide	In or Out	Just Friends
Years 1918															
1931															
1944															
1957															
1970															
Titles Fine Days															
Grey Skies															
High Tide															
In or Out															
Just Friends															
Authors Heddy Heath															
Jim Joyner															
Keith Koch															
Midge Mintz															
Nick Norris															

Years	Borrowers	Authors	Titles
1918			
1931			
1944			
1957			
1970			

Answers on page 183.

Read this account, then turn the page.

Most of us have never heard of Ernesto Miranda. Yet in 1963, this faceless man would prompt the passage of a law that has become an integral part of all arrests. Here's how it came to pass.

In 1963, following his arrest for the kidnapping and rape of an 18-year-old woman, Ernesto Miranda was arrested and placed in a Phoenix, Arizona, police lineup. When he stepped down from the gallery of suspects, Miranda asked the officers about the charges against him. His police captors implied that he had been positively identified as the kidnapper and rapist of a young woman. After two hours of interrogation, Miranda confessed.

Miranda signed a confession that included a typed paragraph indicating that his statement had been voluntary and that he had been fully aware of his legal rights.

But there was one problem: At no time during his interrogation had Miranda actually been advised of his rights. The wheels of justice had been set in motion on a highly unbalanced axle.

When appealing Miranda's conviction, his attorney attempted to have the confession thrown out on the grounds that his client hadn't been advised of his rights. The motion was overruled. Eventually, Miranda would be convicted on both rape and kidnapping charges and sentenced to 20 to 30 years in prison. It seemed like the end of the road for Miranda—but it was just the beginning.

Miranda requested that his case be heard by the U.S. Supreme Court. His attorney, John J. Flynn, submitted a 2,000-word petition [for a writ of *certiorari* (judicial review), arguing that Miranda's Fifth Amendment rights had been violated. In November 1965, the Supreme Court agreed to hear Miranda's case. The tide was about to turn.

After much debate among Miranda's attorneys and the state, a decision in Miranda's favor was rendered. Chief Justice Earl Warren wrote in his *Miranda v. Arizona* opinion, "The person in custody must, prior to interrogation, be clearly informed that he has the right to remain silent, and that anything he says will be used against him in court; he must be clearly informed that he has the right to consult with a lawyer and to have the lawyer with him during interrogation, and that, if he is indigent, a lawyer will be appointed to represent him."

In the wake of the U.S. Supreme Court's ruling, police departments across the nation began to issue the "Miranda warning." As for Miranda himself, his freedom was short-lived. He would be sentenced to 11 years in prison at a second trial that did not include his prior confession as evidence. Miranda was released in 1972, and he bounced in and out of jail for various offenses over the next few years. On January 31, 1976, Miranda was stabbed to death during a Phoenix bar fight. The suspect received his Miranda warning from the arresting police officers and opted to remain silent. Due to insufficient evidence, he would not be prosecuted for Ernesto Miranda's murder.

(Do not read this until you have read the previous page!)

1. Ernesto Miranda was arrested in this year.
   A. 1933
   B. 1936
   C. 1953
   D. 1963

2. Miranda's lawyers argued that these Constitutional rights have been violated.
   A. First Amendment
   B. Fourth Amendment
   C. Fifth Amendment
   D. Sixth Amendment

3. The Chief Justice at the time was this person.
   A. William Rehnquist
   B. Earl Warren
   C. John Roberts
   D. John Marshall

4. Miranda died in prison.
   _____True
   _____False

Answers on page 183.

On Chicago Avenue, there are 5 houses that are identical to each other. You need to follow up with a witness, Jimmy Perez, but without any address on the doors you are not sure which house to approach. You know that from a previous statement that Perez lives with his husband and has no children. The staff at the corner coffee shop and your own observations give you some clues. From the information given, can you find the right house?

A. One staff member says that Perez drives a compact and his husband has an SUV.

B. They do not have a motorcycle but are interested in buying one, and have said they'll get advice from their next door neighbor.

C. Houses A and E have motorcycles in front of them.

D. House B has a minivan parked in front of it and children's toys in the yard.

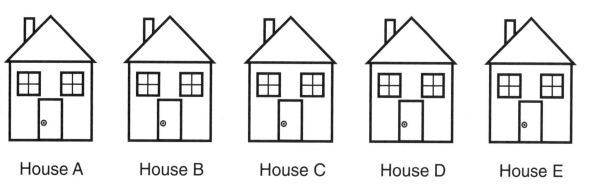

House A   House B   House C   House D   House E

Answers on page 183.

BRAZEN ARMORED CAR HEISTS
(PART 1)

Read these true crime accounts, then turn to the next page to test your knowledge.

The Great Vault Robbery, Jacksonville, Florida: $22 million

In March 1997, 33-year-old Philip Johnson, who made $7 an hour as a driver for armored-car company Loomis Fargo, took off with one of the cars he was supposed to be guarding. Johnson pulled off the caper by waiting until the end of the night, when the armored cars returned to the Loomis Fargo vaults. Johnson tied up the two vault employees, loaded an armored car with about $22 million in cash, and took off.

He remained on the lam for more than four months, despite a half-million-dollar reward for his arrest. He was finally arrested crossing into the United States from Mexico in August 1997.

The majority of the money—which had been stashed in a rental storage unit in rural North Carolina—was recovered shortly afterward.

Dunbar Armored, Los Angeles, California: $18.9 million

Though not technically an armored-car robbery, the 1997 heist of $18.9 million dollars from the Dunbar Armored vaults in Los Angeles, is noteworthy for its meticulous planning and the fact that it is considered the largest armed cash robbery in American history.

The mastermind behind the theft was Dunbar Armored employee Allen Pace III, who used his knowledge of the vault's security system, along with his company keys, to gain access to the loot. Pace and his gang were eventually brought down when one of his cohorts, Eugene Hill, paid for something with a stack of bills banded in a Dunbar wrapper. That, plus a shard of taillight that had been the only piece of evidence left at the scene, was enough for investigators to crack the case. Despite the arrest of Pace and several coconspirators, nearly $10 million of the haul still remains unaccounted for.

Armored Motor Service of America, Rochester, New York: $10.8 million

In June 1990, a driver for the Armored Motor Service of America (AMSA) and his female partner stopped for breakfast at a convenience store near Rochester. While the female guard went into the store, a band of armed thieves attacked the driver, waited for the female guard to return, then ordered them to drive the truck to an unnamed location, where the thieves transferred the money to a waiting van, tied up the two guards, and escaped with the money. The total haul of $10.8 million ranked as one the largest heists in history. The robbery was also noteworthy for the fact that it remained unsolved for more than a decade. In 2002, though, the driver of the robbed AMSA truck, Albert Ranieri, admitted to masterminding the scheme.

Express Teller Services, Columbia, South Carolina: $9.8 million

In 2007, two young men overpowered an Express Teller Services armored car driver when he and his partners stopped to fuel up. They drove the car to a remote area, where two accomplices waited with another vehicle to transfer the cash. The theft of $9.8 million was one of the biggest in American history, but it wasn't particularly well executed. First, the thieves didn't bring a large enough vehicle or enough bags to take the nearly $20 million that was in the truck. Next, the bandits savagely beat one of the guards, while leaving the other one—who was later arrested as the mastermind—untouched. But the gang really did themselves in by going on a weeklong spending spree involving strippers, tattoos, and Mother's Day gifts. Not surprisingly, just about the entire gang was arrested less than a week later.

(Do not read this until you have read the previous page!)

1. Philip Johnson worked in this state.

    A. Florida

    B. North Carolina

    C. California

    D. New York

2. How much money was stolen from Dunbar Armored in Los Angeles by Allen Pace III?

    A. $22 million

    B. About $19 million

    C. About $11 million

    D. About $10 million

3. In the South Carolina theft, the criminals spent some of the stolen money on this.

    A. Drugs

    B. Travel

    C. They didn't have the chance to spend any of it.

    D. Mother's Day gifts

4. In many of these cases, employees and guards hired by the companies were responsible for the thefts.

    _____ True

    _____ False

Answers on page 183.

MOTEL HIDEOUT

A thief hides out in one of the 45 motel rooms listed in the chart below. The motel's in-house detective received a sheet of four clues, signed "The Logical Thief." Using these clues, the detective found the room number within 15 minutes—but by that time, the thief had fled. Can you find the thief's motel room quicker?

1. The second digit is at least twice as large as the first digit.
2. One digit is even and the other is odd.
3. The digits add up to the number 9.
4. The number is not divisible by 6.

51	52	53	54	55	56	57	58	59
41	42	43	44	45	46	47	48	49
31	32	33	34	35	36	37	38	39
21	22	23	24	25	26	27	28	29
11	12	13	14	15	16	17	18	19

Read this true crime account, then turn to the next page to test your knowledge.

Jack Gilbert Graham's mother, Daisie King, knew her only son was no angel, but she must have hoped he'd change his ways: Barely into his 20s, Graham had little patience for lawful employment, and he'd already been convicted of running illegal booze and check forgery. It's thought that King paid for her son's lawyer and anted up $2,500 in court-ordered restitution on the forgery convictions.

By 1953, however, it seemed that Graham was settling down. He married and by 1955 had two children. His mother, a successful businesswoman, bought a house in Colorado for the young couple, built a drive-in restaurant, and installed Graham as its manager.

But the drive-in lost money. Graham blamed his mother's meddling in the management for the loss, but he later admitted he had skimmed receipts. He also confessed to vandalizing the place twice, once by smashing the front window and the second time by rigging a gas explosion to destroy equipment he'd used as security for a personal loan. A new pickup truck Graham bought himself mysteriously stalled on a railway track with predictable results. This too proved to be an attempt at insurance fraud.

In the fall of 1955, King wanted to see her daughter in Alaska, and she prepared for her trip there via Portland and Seattle. On November 1, Graham saw her off on United Air Flight 629. Eleven minutes after takeoff, the plane exploded in the sky. Forty-four people died, including King.

Within 24 hours FBI fingerprint experts were at the crash site to help identify bodies. The painstaking task of gathering wreckage from over a three-mile trail of scraps started. By November 7, Civil Aeronautics investigators concluded sabotage was the probable cause of the disaster.

Criminal investigators joined the FBI technical teams. Families of passengers and crew members were interviewed while technicians reassembled the plane's midsection where the explosion likely occurred. In the course of sifting through wreckage, bomb fragments and explosives residue were identified.

Inevitably, investigators took an interest in Graham. Not only would he receive a substantial inheritance from his mother's estate, he had also taken out a $37,500 travel insurance policy on her. Moreover, he had a criminal record, and according to witnesses, a history of heated arguments with his mother.

Graham was first interviewed on November 10, and again over the following two days. In a search of his property on November 12, agents discovered a roll of primer cord in a shirt pocket and a copy of the travel insurance policy secreted in a small box. Circumstantial evidence contradicted his statements, including that provided by his wife, half-sister, and acquaintances.

Finally, Graham admitted he'd built a bomb and placed it in his mother's luggage. On November 14, he was arraigned on charges of sabotage. At the time the charge did not carry a death penalty, so he was brought back into court on November 17 and charged with first-degree murder.

Notwithstanding the confession, investigators continued to gather forensic evidence, putting together what may have been the most scientifically detailed case in U.S. history up to that date. The case had other firsts as well. It was the first case of mass murder in the United States via airplane explosion. Graham's trial, which began on April 16, 1956, also marked the first time TV cameras were permitted to air a live broadcast of a courtroom trial.

On May 5, 1956, the jury needed only 69 minutes to find Graham guilty. On January 11, 1957, he was executed at Colorado State Penitentiary, remorseless to the end.

(Do not read this until you have read the previous page!)

1. Graham managed this kind of business, which his mother bought for him.
   - A. Drive-in movie theater
   - B. Drive-in restaurant
   - C. Gas station
   - D. Bar

2. Graham's crimes prior to 1955 included:
   - A. Check forgery
   - B. Vandalism
   - C. Insurance fraud
   - D. All of the above

3. Graham had taken out a travel insurance policy on his mother for this amount.
   - A. $5,600
   - B. $18,800
   - C. $37,500
   - D. $100,000

4. Graham's trial was the first in the U.S. to be broadcast live.
   - _____True
   - _____False

Answers on page 184.

Cryptograms are messages in substitution code. Break the code to read the message. For example, THE SMART CAT might become FVO QWGDF JGF if **F** is substituted for **T, V** for **H, O** for **E,** and so on.

PBCO MQPZB KWCIPRN DRAWI WO WI WNPCOP JT JNCACIWG UJNF, AWCICIA OJHR OQZZROO. BJURSRN, BCO UJNF UWO OJHRPCHRO ZNCPCLQRM WO MRNCSWPCSR WIM QIJNCACIWG. BR RSRIPQWGGX PQNIRM PJ TJNARNCRO, CIZGQMCIA JT MQPZB KWCIPRN EJBWIIRO SRNHRRN. MQNCIA UJNGM UWN CC, JIR JT PBR TJNARN'O KWCIPCIAO RIMRM QK CI PBR BWIMO JT IWYC BRNHWI AJNCIA. SWI HRRARNWI UWO WNNROPRM WTPRN PBR UWN TJN ZJGGWDJNWPCJI UCPB PBR RIRHX—QIPCG BR RVKGWCIRM PBWP BR BWMI'P OJGM W NRWG SRNHRRN, DQP W TJNARNX. BR UWO ACSRI W GROORN ORIPRIZR TJN TNWQM, PBJQAB BR MCRM DRTJNR BR ORNSRM PCHR CI KNCOJI.

In the 1800s, William Burke and William Hare were two men supplying cadavers for anatomical study to Dr. Robert Knox. They eventually began killing people in order to receive extra payment. Every word listed is contained within the group of letters. Words can be found in a straight line horizontally, vertically, or diagonally. They may be read either forward or backward.

ANATOMY

CADAVERS

CORPSES

DISSECTION

EDINBURGH

GRAVE ROBBING

LODGERS

MARGARET DOCHERTY (final victim)

MEDICAL RESEARCH

MURDER

RESURRECTION MEN

ROBERT KNOX

SCOTLAND

SIXTEEN VICTIMS

SUFFOCATION

WILLIAM BURKE

WILLIAM HARE

```
S  U  F  F  O  C  A  T  I  O  N  S  R  O  Y  S  N  S  D
W  I  L  L  I  A  M  B  U  R  K  E  S  G  R  A  O  Y  Z
E  T  J  V  I  W  M  E  D  I  N  B  U  R  G  H  I  Y  X
F  S  C  A  K  W  E  G  X  Q  K  O  M  U  U  T  T  R  B
R  M  I  B  G  X  D  N  N  S  O  N  S  Z  R  C  N  J
E  I  I  D  Y  X  I  D  I  I  F  R  L  T  E  P  E  E  Q
R  T  L  J  N  F  C  G  C  Z  B  M  E  H  G  O  S  M  S
A  C  O  O  C  T  A  I  M  X  U  B  C  G  J  P  S  N  R
H  I  O  N  J  A  L  P  P  C  Q  O  O  J  D  F  I  O  E
M  V  N  R  I  C  R  M  U  R  D  E  R  R  G  O  D  I  V
A  N  R  X  P  H  E  D  O  T  U  Q  L  C  E  E  L  T  A
I  E  N  F  D  S  S  B  E  D  K  N  Y  J  D  V  J  C  D
L  E  H  R  F  E  E  R  Y  Y  A  A  X  N  C  D  A  E  A
L  T  A  L  N  R  A  S  D  R  C  Z  A  U  F  Y  C  R  C
I  X  X  Q  T  G  R  H  Z  L  K  L  J  G  T  T  X  R  G
W  I  X  K  R  O  C  R  W  E  T  U  V  H  Z  K  Q  U  N
Q  S  N  A  S  O  H  K  W  O  W  X  W  X  P  K  W  S  I
L  O  M  Y  Q  I  V  J  C  Y  M  O  T  A  N  A  U  E  U
X  X  C  N  Y  W  K  S  X  X  M  Y  A  R  O  X  P  R  M
```

Read this true crime account, then turn to the next page to test your knowledge.

So-called "black widows"—women who marry and then kill their spouses and sometimes families for profit—stand out for their sheer unlikelihood as perpetrators. The black widows that follow got caught up in their own webs.

Artiste of Arsenic

Norwegian immigrant Belle Poulsdatter (b. 1859), known as the Black Widow of the Heartland, was married for 17 years before her husband died and she collected $8,000 in life insurance. Belle moved her family to LaPorte, Indiana, where she later married wealthy widower Peter Gunness, who died when a meat grinder tumbled from a high shelf and landed on his head. His death was ruled accidental, and Belle collected Peter's insurance money and his estate.

Belle advertised for farmhands in a newspaper that catered to incoming Norwegian immigrants. Of those who responded, Belle hired the ones who came with a sturdy bank account as well as a sturdy back. Laborers came and went—and some simply disappeared.

When the Gunness farmhouse burned to the ground in 1908, the bodies of Belle's children and an unidentified headless female were found in the cellar. A search of the property revealed the bodies of Belle's suitors and laborers buried in the hog pen, some killed by arsenic, some by skull trauma. The widow was nowhere to be found. Belle's remaining beau-cum-farmhand was convicted of murdering Belle and her family. However, the identity of the headless corpse was never conclusive, leading some to believe that Belle staged the entire thing and escaped.

The Giggling Grandmother

From the mid-1920s to the mid-'50s, Nannie Doss left a trail of corpses: her mother, two sisters, a nephew, and a grandson. A mother of four trapped in an unhappy marriage, Nannie also murdered two of her children with rat poison before her first husband left her. She collected on the children's life insurance policies. Nannie married three more times, but each husband contracted a mysterious stomach ailment and died, leaving his widow his insurance settlement, home, and estate.

Coincidentally, Nannie's fifth husband also died of a stomach ailment. His physician ordered an autopsy, which showed a significant amount of rat poison. After her arrest, the bodies of her former spouses were exhumed for examination; all showed traces of poison. Nannie giggled as she confessed her crimes to the police, earning her the nickname, "The Giggling Grandmother."

Nobody Buys the Doppelgänger Bit

Frank Hilley had been married to Marie for more than 20 years when he was admitted to the hospital with stomach pain and diagnosed with acute infectious hepatitis in 1975. He died within the month, and Marie collected on his life insurance policy. Three years later, she took out a life insurance policy on her daughter Carol, whereupon Carol developed a strange illness with symptoms of nausea and numbness in her extremities. Physicians detected an abnormal level of arsenic in Carol's system and suspected foul play. Frank's body was exhumed and tests revealed that he had died of arsenic poisoning.

Marie was arrested in October 1979 for the attempted murder of her daughter, but was released on bond a month later. She promptly disappeared. Despite her indictment for murder, Marie remained a fugitive for more than three years before marrying John Homan in Florida under the alias Robbi Hannon.

In a bizarre turn of events, Marie invented a twin sister, "Teri," staged "Robbi's" death, and then returned to her husband pretending to be her grief-stricken twin, Teri. The ruse was discovered, and Marie was sent to Alabama, where she was wanted on other charges. The house of cards fell apart, and she was convicted of murder and attempted murder and sentenced to life in prison. Marie served four years of her sentence before she escaped during a furlough. She was found days later, freezing and wandering in the woods near Anniston, Alabama. Marie was admitted to the hospital, where she died of hypothermia.

(Do not read this until you have read the previous page!)

1. Belle Poulsdatter was married to her first husband for:

    A. 1 year

    B. 5 years

    C. 17 years

    D. 23 years

2. Belle used this poison.

    A. Arsenic

    B. Cyanide

    C. Rat poison

    D. Prussic acid

3. How many husbands did Nannie Doss have?

    A. 3

    B. 4

    C. 5

    D. 7

4. Marie Hilley used this poison against her husband and daughter.

    A. Arsenic

    B. Cyanide

    C. Rat poison

    D. Prussic acid

Answers on page 184.

Study this picture of the crime scene for 1 minute, then turn the page.

(Do not read this until you have read the previous page!) Which image exactly matches the picture from the previous page?

1.

2.

3.

4.

Answers on page 185.

Cryptograms are messages in substitution code. Break the code to read the message. For example, THE SMART CAT might become FVO QWGDF JGF if **F** is substituted for **T, V** for **H, O** for **E,** and so on.

RJG BNURFHZ VUQ IJMH FH CJHOJH FH 1914. FH DFQ XJSRD, DN VJMBNO PJM DFQ PUGFCX UQ U KUFHRNM JP DJSQNQ. CURNM, UPRNM RDN QNEJHO VJMCO VUM, DN VNHR RJ EJCCNZN RJ QRSOX UMR. UCRDJSZD DN OMJKKNO JSR, DN QRSOFNO VFRD QNTNMUC UMR MNQRJMNMQ. DN RDNH INZUH RJ PJMZN UHO QNCC VJMBQ JP UMR. DJVNTNM, BNURFHZ RNHONO RJ CNUTN ECSNQ FH RDN KUFHRFHZ RDUR RDNX VNMN PJMZNMFNQ. DN ECUFGNO RJ KNMENFTN DFQ PJMZNMFNQ UQ HJR QJ GSED UH FHRNHR RJ ONPMUSO ISR UQ U VUX RJ EMFRFLSN RDN EJMMSKRFJH JP RDN UMR VJMCO. DN ECUFGNO RJ DUTN KUFHRNO GJMN RDUH 2,000 PJMZNMFNQ.

Answers on page 185.

Samuel Green (1796–1822) was called America's first "Public Enemy Number One." He terrorized New England with his occasional accomplice William Ash. Every word listed is contained within the group of letters. Words can be found in a straight line horizontally, vertically, or diagonally. They may be read either forward or backward.

BURGLARY

CANADA

COUNTERFEITING

DEATH BY HANGING

ESCAPE

FRANKLIN LOOMIS (mentor)

GALLOWS

NEW HAMPSHIRE

PRISON

PUBLIC ENEMY

ROBBERY

SERIAL KILLER

"TERROR OF NEW ENGLAND" (nickname)

WILLIAM ASH

```
G O K J R B O H T O M Y B M E M O B Y
I C Y B U E Y G S Y R Z D R L G M V T
S L T O V K L D G A X S T Q L T Y H E
Z D B I X G W L L V M N A D A N A C R
C E S W E H F G I O V A R E E W X D R
O A W F J E R C I K H P I W A N W K O
U T O R L U Q D F O L P H L P C M Q R
N H L A B A K E K E S A P C L V H M O
T B L N H K H Q V I M U I V T I Y C F
E Y A K P I V I U P B T M R L U W W N
R H G L T K M P S L G V D A E M C V E
F A L I S P Y H I Y Q J X X V S X Z W
E N Q N W D I C Z Q Y T N O S I R P E
I G P L K R E Z C U Y M Q K R Z O F N
T I C O E N N T V K Q Q S O Y C B F G
I N D O E V E V Z U L P K H T R B U L
N G H M A T G D J H Y G K R Y U E F A
G P Y I B D B A V R E N S B A K R A N
Q S F S M V X E P A C S E S Q W Y D D
```

Answers on page 185.

A thief hides out in one of the 45 motel rooms listed in the chart below. The motel's in-house detective received a sheet of four clues, signed "The Logical Thief." Using these clues, the detective found the room number within 15 minutes—but by that time, the thief had fled. Can you find the thief's motel room quicker?

1. The number is divisible by 3.

2. The digits add up to 6.

3. Both digits are prime numbers.

4. The first number is larger than the second.

51	52	53	54	55	56	57	58	59
41	42	43	44	45	46	47	48	49
31	32	33	34	35	36	37	38	39
21	22	23	24	25	26	27	28	29
11	12	13	14	15	16	17	18	19

        Answers on page 185.

Read the story below, than turn the page and answer the questions.

The detective overheard the jewelry thief tell her accomplice about the different places where she stashed the loot. She said, "The gold bars are in a sack in the treehouse at the farm. The diamonds are taped to a closed vent in the front room of the Chicago two-flat. The ruby choker is in a sack of flour in the pantry at the condo. The emeralds are in the safety deposit box at the bank on Fourth Street."

(Do not read this until you have read the previous page!)

The investigator overheard the information about where the stolen loot was stored, but didn't have anywhere to write it down! Answer the questions below to help the investigator remember.

1. What is found in a treehouse?

   A. Gold bars

   B. Diamonds

   C. Rubies

   D. Emeralds

2. What is found in a sack of flour?

   A. Ruby bracelet

   B. Ruby choker

   C. Ruby ring

   D. Emeralds

3. The diamonds are found in this building.

   A. Farmhouse

   B. Two-flat

   C. Condo

   D. Bank

4. The bank is found here.

   A. Fourth Street

   B. Fourth Avenue

   C. Fourth Drive

   D. We are not told.

Answers on page 186.

Read this true crime account, then turn to the next page to test your knowledge.

Richard Loeb and Nathan Leopold grew up in the Kenwood neighborhood in Chicago, Illinois. Loeb's father was a Sears, Roebuck & Co. vice president, Leopold's was a wealthy box manufacturer. Loeb was obsessed with crime novels, and Leopold was obsessed with Loeb—and with the idea of Nietzsche's superman, a superior individual who was above the law and could do as he pleased. Leopold believed that a superman could even commit murder. When Loeb conceived of the idea to attempt a perfect crime—one for which they would never be caught—Leopold was his willing accomplice.

In 1924—when Loeb was 18 and Leopold was 19—the two lured Loeb's 14-year-old cousin Bobby Franks into a car and beat the unsuspecting child to death. They attempted to hide the body near Wolf Lake; they did a poor job, however, and a passerby found the body the next day. Investigators then discovered Leopold's glasses in the area where the body was found, and the boys were quickly apprehended.

The trial was a sensation; because the boys had pleaded guilty, the main point of the trial was to determine if the boys would go to prison or be hanged. Defense attorney Clarence Darrow claimed that both boys were mentally unstable because they had been abused by their governesses; using this defense among others, Darrow persuaded the judge to spare the boys' lives, much to prosecutor Robert Crowe's chagrin.

Loeb was killed in prison in 1936. Leopold was a model prisoner and was released in 1958. Even prosecutor Robert Crowe had become convinced of Leopold's reform and considered writing a letter to the parole board on his behalf. Leopold lived most of the rest of his life in Puerto Rico. He died in 1971.

Bobby Franks is buried in Rosehill Cemetery. Some cemetery workers claimed to see a young boy wandering the cemetery at times; when they approached him, he would disappear, however. The workers claimed the ghost did not rest until Leopold's death in 1971.

Answers on page 186.

(Do not read this until you have read the previous page!)

1. The Leopold/Loeb murder took place in this decade.
   A. 1910s
   B. 1920s
   C. 1930s
   D. 1940s

2. Their victim was...
   A. Loeb's cousin
   B. Leopold's cousin
   C. A neighborhood kid, but no relation
   D. A stranger passing through town

3. Clarence Darrow, of the Scopes monkey trial, played this role.
   A. Defense attorney
   B. Prosecutor
   C. Judge
   D. Special Counsel

4. Both men died in prison.
   _____ True
   _____ False

Answers on page 186.

Study this picture for 1 minute, then turn the page.

(Do not read this until you have read the previous page!) Which image exactly matches the picture from the previous page?

1.

2.

3.

4.

Answers on page 186.

On Washington Street, there are 5 houses. You need to follow up with a witness, Jennifer Brown, but without any address on the doors you are not sure which house to approach. You know that from a previous statement that Brown lives with her husband and stepdaughter. The staff at the corner coffee shop and your own observations give you some clues. From the information given, can you find the right house?

A. The Browns recently repainted their house white, like two other homes on their street.

B. There are two houses with kids living in them, and they are not adjacent.

C. House D is green and house C is blue.

D. House A has two kids living in it.

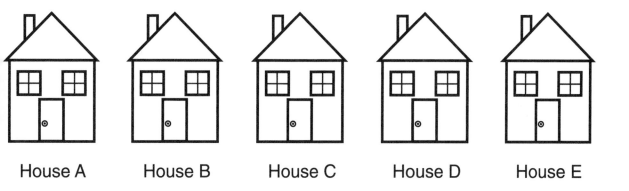

House A   House B   House C   House D   House E

Answers on page 186.

POLICE DISPATCHER

Trevor was on-call today as the Libertyville Police Department's primary dispatcher. He received six calls during the morning shift, each from a different part of town, and each for a different reason (such as a stolen car or a bank robbery). He dispatched a different officer for each of these six calls. Using only the clues below, help him sort out his dispatch log by matching each call to its time, location, and assigned officer.

1. Of Brenda and whoever was dispatched to deal with the alarm, one went Downtown and the other was sent to the North End.

2. Harry didn't leave at 11:45am.

3. One officer was dispatched to the scene of a truck accident 3 hours after the call to go Downtown.

4. Jeffrey was sent out sometime after the Midtown call.

5. Of Neville and whoever went to investigate the stolen car, one was dispatched at 10:15am and the other went to Midtown.

6. One officer (who wasn't Linda) was sent to check on a cat stuck in a tree 45 minutes before another was sent to the North End.

7. The 10:15am call, Harry's call, the one for the South End, and the one for the bank robbery involved four different officers.

8. Brenda headed out sometime after whoever went Uptown. The Uptown dispatch didn't happen at either 8:45am or 10:15am.

9. The officer that went to the South End left 2 hours and 15 minutes after whoever went to the scene of the bank robbery.

10. Neither Dale nor Linda was dispatched to investigate the trespassing call.

	Officers						Calls						Locations					
	Brenda	Dale	Harry	Jeffrey	Linda	Neville	Accident	Alarm	Bank robbery	Cat in tree	Stolen car	Trespassing	Bus. District	Downtown	Midtown	North End	South End	Uptown
8:45am																		
9:30am																		
10:15am																		
11:00am																		
11:45am																		
12:30pm																		
Bus. District																		
Downtown																		
Midtown																		
North End																		
South End																		
Uptown																		
Accident																		
Alarm																		
Bank robbery																		
Cat in tree																		
Stolen car																		
Trespassing																		

Times	Officers	Calls	Locations
8:45am			
9:30am			
10:15am			
11:00am			
11:45am			
12:30pm			

Answers on page 186.

Every word listed is contained within the group of letters. Words can be found in a straight line horizontally, vertically, or diagonally. They may be read either forward or backward.

A IS FOR ACID

FOXCATCHER

THE IMPOSTER

THE JINX

THE KILLING SEASON

MAKING A MURDERER

A MURDER IN THE PARK

SERIAL

THE SEVEN FIVE

THE THIN BLUE LINE

TOWER

THE WIDOWER

THE WITNESS

```
R  N  A  E  Y  D  K  Y  V  A  A  T  E  C  D  E  Q
E  O  M  P  Z  P  M  Q  Q  T  S  E  A  S  J  N  W
R  S  U  X  A  H  I  Q  T  H  P  V  B  R  W  I  E
E  A  R  N  F  H  F  X  O  E  G  A  U  V  R  L  Z
D  E  D  I  O  T  H  E  W  I  D  O  W  E  R  E  T
R  S  E  J  X  V  Q  T  E  M  R  U  R  E  L  U  H
U  G  R  E  C  H  O  R  R  P  E  O  X  V  C  L  E
M  N  I  H  A  Q  V  F  R  O  I  H  U  I  H  B  W
A  I  N  T  T  O  L  C  D  S  M  H  M  F  O  N  I
G  L  T  J  C  H  O  A  R  T  V  I  G  N  Q  I  T
N  L  H  Q  H  M  G  F  I  E  Z  K  P  E  A  H  N
I  I  E  S  E  V  L  U  E  R  C  S  E  V  E  T  E
K  K  P  J  R  W  F  A  M  Z  E  K  N  E  X  E  S
A  E  A  C  X  K  Y  V  A  K  H  S  N  S  X  H  S
M  H  R  N  F  I  R  E  D  B  A  M  O  E  V  T  Q
T  T  K  H  V  A  Z  N  C  L  U  N  P  H  S  J  N
K  E  D  A  I  S  F  O  R  A  C  I  D  T  D  E  L
```

135   Answers on page 187.

Read this true crime account, then turn to the next page to test your knowledge.

Meet the two charming fellows who inspired the children's rhyme: "Burke's the Butcher, Hare's the Thief, Knox the boy that buys the beef."

In the 1820s, Edinburgh, Scotland, was suffering from a "cadaver crunch." Considering the city was regarded as a center of medical education, the lack of bodies for students to dissect in anatomy classes posed a problem. At the time, there were strict limits on the use of bodies for medical research, primarily those executed for crimes. Interestingly, at the same time that enrollment in medical schools was rising (as well as the need for cadavers), the number of executions was decreasing. This was due to the repeal of the so-called "Bloody Code," which by 1815 listed more than 200 capital offenses.

The growing need for corpses created a grisly new occupation. "Resurrection Men" dug up the newly buried dead and sold the bodies to medical schools. William Burke and William Hare decided to cut out the middleman: Over the course of a year, they murdered at least 15 people in order to sell their bodies.

The pair fell into the cadaver supply business on November 29, 1827. At the time, Hare was running a cheap boarding house in an Edinburgh slum. Burke was his tenant and drinking buddy. When one of Hare's tenants died still owing four pounds, Hare and Burke stole the tenant's corpse from his coffin and sold it to recover the back rent. Dr. Robert Knox, who taught anatomy to 500 students at Edinburgh Medical College, paid more than seven pounds for the body.

Encouraged by the profit, Burke and Hare looked for other bodies to sell to Knox. Their first victim was another tenant at the boarding house, who fell ill a few days later. Burke and Hare "comforted" the sick man with whiskey until he passed out, and then smothered him. The result was a body that looked like it had died of drunkenness, with no marks of foul play.

Over the course of the next year, Burke and Hare lured more victims into the lodging house. They sold the bodies to Knox, who not only accepted them without question, but increased the pair's payment to ten pounds because of the "freshness" of the bodies they provided.

Their initial targets were strangers to Edinburgh, but Burke and Hare soon began to take more risks, murdering local prostitutes and "Daft Jamie," a well-known neighborhood character. People began to talk about the disappearances, and Knox's students began to recognize the bodies brought to them for dissection.

Burke and Hare's mercenary killings ended on October 31, 1828, when Burke lured an old Irish woman named Mary Docherty to the house. James and Ann Gray, who were also boarders at the time, met Docherty there. Docherty was invited to spend the night, and arrangements were made for the Grays to board elsewhere. The next morning, the Grays returned and found the old woman's body under the bed. Although they were offered a bribe of ten pounds a week to keep quiet, the Grays ran for the police.

Hare testified against Burke in exchange for immunity. He was released in February 1829 and disappeared from the historical record, though popular legend claims he ended his life a blind beggar on the streets of London. Burke was tried for murder, found guilty, and hung. Although there was no evidence that Knox had any knowledge of the murders, angry crowds appeared at his lectures and tore his effigy to shreds. He eventually moved to London.

Fittingly, Burke's corpse was turned over to the Edinburgh Medical College for "useful dissection." A bit more oddly, skin from his body was used to bind a small book.

The murders led to the passage of the Anatomy Act of 1832, which provided new legal sources for medical cadavers and eliminated the profit motive that drove Burke and Hare to murder.

(Do not read this until you have read the previous page!)

1. Burke and Hare murdered at least this many people.

   A. 3

   B. 5

   C. 10

   D. 15

2. Hare ran this type of establishment

   A. Pub

   B. Boarding house

   C. Orphanage

   D. Cemetary

3. Burke and Hare were caught because:

   A. A victim got away and called the police.

   B. A couple found the body of a victim.

   C. Burke turned against Hare.

   D. The doctor buying the bodies became suspicious.

4. Hare's body was used for dissection after he was executed.

   _____ True

   _____ False

Answers on page 187.

MOTEL HIDEOUT

A thief hides out in one of the 45 motel rooms listed in the chart below. The motel's in-house detective received a sheet of four clues, signed "The Logical Thief." Using these clues, the detective found the room number within 15 minutes—but by that time, the thief had fled. Can you find the thief's motel room quicker?

1. Each digit is a prime number.

2. The number itself is not prime.

3. The second digit is larger than the first digit by 2.

4. The sum of the digits is less than 10.

51	52	53	54	55	56	57	58	59
41	42	43	44	45	46	47	48	49
31	32	33	34	35	36	37	38	39
21	22	23	24	25	26	27	28	29
11	12	13	14	15	16	17	18	19

Answers on page 187.

Read this true crime account, then turn to the next page to test your knowledge.

The sensational crime captured the public imagination of late-19th-century America. On the morning of August 4, 1892, in Fall River, Massachusetts, the bodies of Andrew Borden and his second wife, Abby, were found slaughtered in the home they shared with an Irish maid, Bridget, and Andrew's 32-year-old daughter, Lizzie. A second daughter, Emma, was away from home at the time.

Although Lizzie was a devout, church-going Sunday school teacher, she was charged with the horrific murders and was immortalized in the rhyme: "Lizzie Borden took an ax and gave her mother 40 whacks. When she saw what she had done, she gave her father 41." In reality, her stepmother was struck 19 times, killed in an upstairs bedroom with the same ax that crushed her husband's skull while he slept on a couch downstairs. In that gruesome attack, his face took 11 blows.

Andrew was one of the wealthiest men in Fall River. By reputation, he was also one of the meanest. The prosecution alleged that Lizzie's motivation for the murders was financial: She had hoped to inherit her father's estate.

Despite the large quantity of blood at the crime scene, the police were unable to find any blood-soaked clothing worn by Lizzie when she allegedly committed the crimes. However, several things pointed to Lizzie as the likeliest murderer. Lizzie appeared to be the only one in the house at the time, other than Bridget. She showed no signs of grief when the murders were discovered. Just a day before the murders, Lizzie had been attempting to purchase prussic acid—a deadly poison—and the family came down with "food poisoning" that night. During questioning, Lizzie changed her story several times. The evidence was entirely circumstantial, but it was compelling enough to go to trial.

Lizzie's defense counsel successfully had their client's contradictory inquest testimony ruled inadmissible, along with all evidence relating to her earlier attempts to purchase poison from a local drugstore. On June 19, 1893, the jury in the case returned its verdict of not guilty. Lizzie went free, and no one else was charged with the crimes.

Who else could have done it? If Lizzie did do it, why? Many theories abounded.

There is no real evidence to support this claim, but some say Andrew had an illegitimate son named William, who may have spent time as an inmate in an insane asylum. At least one witness reportedly saw William at the Borden house on the day of the murders. William was supposedly there to challenge Andrew about his new will.

One of the most curious explanations for the murder involves the Bordens' servant Bridget Sullivan. During the time Abby was being murdered, Bridget was apparently washing windows in the back of the house. Later, when Andrew was killed, Bridget was resting in her room upstairs. Why didn't she hear two people being butchered?

According to some theories, Lizzie and Bridget had been romantically involved. In this version of the story, their relationship was discovered shortly before the murders. Around this same time, Andrew was reportedly rewriting his will. His wife was now "Mrs. Borden," to Lizzie, not "Mother," as Lizzie had called her stepmother for many years. The reason for the estrangement was never clear. Some speculate that Bridget was Lizzie's accomplice in the murders and helped clean up the blood afterward.

This theory was bolstered when, a few years after the murders, Lizzie became involved with actress Nance O'Neil. This prompted Emma Borden, Lizzie's sister, to move out of their home. At the time, the rift between the sisters sparked rumors that either Lizzie or Emma might reveal more about the other's role in the 1892 murders. However, neither of them said anything new about the killings.

Lizzie wasn't the only one with motive, means, and opportunity. The most likely suspects were family members, working alone or with other relatives. Only a few had solid alibis, and—like Lizzie—many changed their stories during police questioning. But there was never enough evidence to officially accuse anyone other than Lizzie.

LIZZIE BORDEN DID WHAT? (PART II)

(Do not read this until you have read the previous page!)

1. Lizzie's sister Emma was here when the crime occurred.
   A. In her room, sleeping
   B. Away from home
   C. On the back porch, cleaning
   D. On the front porch, reading

2. Lizzie had tried to purchase this on the day before the murders.
   A. Arsenic
   B. Cyanide
   C. Prussic acid
   D. An axe

3. Lizzie was the only person ever charged with the crime.
   _____ True
   _____ False

4. Andrew and Abby Borden were killed in their bedroom.
   _____ True
   _____ False

142

Answers on page 187.

Cryptograms are messages in substitution code. Break the code to read the message. For example, THE SMART CAT might become FVO QWGDF JGF if **F** is substituted for **T,** **V** for **H,** **O** for **E,** and so on.

DK RCA QATAKRAAKRC OAKRSPX, E JEK KEJAU
RCLJEQ IHLLU ZEJLSQHX RPDAU RL QRAEH RCA OPLVK
FAVAHQ LZ AKBHEKU ZPLJ RCADP RDBCRHX BSEPUAU
HLOERDLK ER RCA RLVAP LZ HLKULK. IHLLU ZDPQR
OEQAU RCA FLDKR; CA EKU E VLJEK MPARAKUDKB
RL IA CDQ VDZA TDQDRAU RCA RLVAP RL QAA RCA
FAVAHQ, DKBPERDERDKB RCAJQAHTAQ VDRC RCA
OSQRLUDEK. EZRAP QATAPEH TDQDRQ, IHLLU IPLSBCR
QLJA ZPDAKUQ RL QAA RCA FAVAHQ. RCA JAK RCAK
QRPSOG ULVK EKU ILSKU RCA GAAMAP LZ RCA FAVAHQ
EKU ERRAJMRAU RL EIQOLKU VDRC RCA FAVAHQ
RCAJQAHTAQ. DR VEQ E JAQQX RCAZR, EQ RCA JAK
ZHERRAKAU E OPLVK EKU ZDHAU E QOAMRAP DK RVL
DK LPUAP RL QREQC RCAJ IARRAP IAKAERC OHLRCAQ.
RCAX VAPA OESBCR LK ERRAJMRDKB RL ZHAA. LUUHX,
IHLLU VEQ MEPULKAU IX RCA GDKB CDJQAHZ—
MALMHA QMAOSHERAU RCER CA EUJDPAU IHLLU'Q
UEPDKB—EKU ATAK BPEKRAU EK AQRERA.

Answers on page 188.

CRIMES

Every word listed is contained within the group of letters. Words can be found in a straight line horizontally, vertically, or diagonally. They may be read either forward or backward.

ARSON

ASSAULT

BATTERY

BLACKMAIL

BURGLARY

CONSPIRACY

CORRUPTION

EXTORTION

FORGERY

FRAUD

HOMICIDE

KIDNAPPING

LARCENY

MANSLAUGHTER

MURDER

PERJURY

RACKETEERING

ROBBERY

TAX EVASION

THEFT

TRESPASS

```
D N Z O P G Y W V A Y R A S S A U L T W K
I O O C U W Z W T R H P N H L T N L P J T
L N M I M L Z C E U G P E R J U R Y Z B H
H C O W T D L T Q L X N T D A I R V P O O
I M N I R P T C O N S P I R A C Y F S S M
Q W E F S A U W T Y F H S P E F D X H C I
C Y F X B A L R R P K O L W P S R M Y G C
T C N N I V E R N N I A A L A P A E H I
R Y Z T E G B E A O P N R Z R T N A U J D
D N R N P B N C X C C K P X M C V D S D E
M S Z A O F E S W A H Z W M H U E K I S M
D O T R L E X T O R T I O N F H Q N O K B
E M J B F G G P O D E X J J J A R D Y L J
B Q Q M L A R K S O C J S Y W M A N A H D
E M A N S L A U G H T E R V O U L C M L Y
N V K Z C N T R B P F H G O Q B K Y F R M
L S Z G T Z A J E U I E E Z J M W Q E O E
R U L P K O J W P X K D C F A B F G S X H
B R A C K E T E E R I N G I T N R K D Q T
B O G Z D Z O L F G S C L K G O L M Q L B
Z H T U R A M U R D E R J D F S Y I Q K Z
```

145

Answers on page 188.

Match each criminal's name in the left column to his or her nickname in the right column.

1. Harry Hayward

2. Thomas Neill Cream

3. Stephen Richards

4. Elizabeth Bathory

5. Mary Frith

6. Monica Proietti

A. The Blood Countess

B. The Minneapolis Svengali

C. Machine Gun Molly

D. The Nebraska Fiend

E. Moll Cutpurse

F. The Lambeth Poisoner

Answers on page 188.

Read the story below, than turn the page and answer the questions.

The detective overheard the jewelry thief tell his accomplice about the different places where he stashed the loot. He said, "The jade figurine is in a box of old magazines in the basement. The ruby is in the pocket of the bathrobe in the closet. The emeralds are in the dining room hutch inside the water pitcher. The opals are underneath the mattress of the bed in the spare room."

(Do not read this until you have read the previous page!)
The investigator overheard the information about where the stolen loot was stored, but didn't have anywhere to write it down! Answer the questions below to help the investigator remember.

1. How many rubies are there?

    A. 1

    B. 2

    C. 3

    D. More than 1, but we don't know how many.

2. What is found in a box of old magazines?

    A. Jade necklace

    B. Jade figurine

    C. Emeralds

    D. Opals

3. The emeralds are found inside this.

    A. Bathrobe pocket

    B. Water pitcher

    C. Butter dish

    D. Carved box

4. The opals are found here.

    A. Spare room

    B. Dining room

    C. Basement

    D. Closet

Answers on page 189.

Cryptograms are messages in substitution code. Break the code to read the message. For example, THE SMART CAT might become FVO QWGDF JGF if **F** is substituted for **T, V** for **H, O** for **E,** and so on.

UQXO UXM MOHDGF AF OQG MH-TXDDGP QGAMO
HK OQG TGFORLY? PAXEHFPM, ILAEXLADY, UAOQ
MHEG NHDP XFP BGUGDLY KHL NHHP EGXMRLG. OQG
OHOXD TXEG OH EHLG OQXF HFG QRFPLGP EADDAHF
PHDDXLM. OQG NHHPM UGLG MOHDGF KLHE OQG
XFOUGLI UHLDP PAXEHFP TGFOLG AF VGDNARE. OQG
OQAGK GMOXVDAMQGP QAEMGDK XM X OGFXFO OH
OQG VRADPAFN, GFXVDAFN QAM XTTGMM OH OQG
SXRDO. QG UXM TXRNQO VXMGP HF X MXFPUATQ
DGKO FGXL OQG TLAEG MTGFG. OQG PAXEHFPM,
QHUGSGL, UGLG FHO LGTHSGLGP.

Answers on page 189.

Read this account of a (potential) true crime, then turn to the next page to test your knowledge.

Film mogul Thomas Ince joins other Hollywood notables for a weekend celebration in 1924 and ends up dead. Was it natural causes or one of the biggest cover-ups in Hollywood history?

The movie industry has been rocked by scandal throughout its history, but few incidents have matched the controversy and secrecy surrounding the death of Thomas Ince, a high-profile producer and director of many successful silent films. During the 1910s, he set up his own studio in California where he built a sprawling complex of small homes, sweeping mansions, and other buildings that were used as sets for his movies. Known as Inceville, the studio covered several thousand acres, and it was there that Ince perfected the idea of the studio system—a factory-style setup that used a division of labor amongst large teams of costumers, carpenters, electricians, and other film professionals who moved from project to project as needed. This system, which allowed for the mass production of movies with the producer in creative and financial control, would later be adopted by all major Hollywood film companies.

Down on his luck by the 1920s, Ince still had many influential friends and associates. In November 1924, newspaper magnate William Randolph Hearst offered to host a weekend birthday celebration for the struggling producer aboard his luxury yacht the *Oneida.* Several Hollywood luminaries attended, including Charlie Chaplin and Marion Davies, as well Louella Parsons, then a junior writer for one of Hearst's East Coast newspapers. But at the end of the cruise, Ince was carried off the ship on a medical gurney and rushed home, where he died two days later. A hastily scribbled death certificate blamed heart failure.

Almost immediately, the rumor mill churned out shocking and sordid versions of the incident, which were very different from the official line. A Chaplin employee, who was waiting at the docks when the boat returned, reportedly claimed that Ince was suffering from a gunshot wound to the head when he was taken off the *Oneida.* Could he have been the victim of a careless accident at the hands of a partying Hollywood celeb? Perhaps, but film industry insiders knew of complex and passionate relationships among those on board, and a convoluted and bizarre scenario soon emerged and has persisted to this day. As it turns out, Davies was Hearst's longtime nistress, despite being almost 34 years his junior. She was also a close friend of the notorious womanizer Chaplin. Many speculate that Hearst, enraged over the attention that Chaplin was paying to the young ingenue, set out to kill him but shot the hapless Ince by mistake.

Certain events after Ince's death helped the rumors gain traction. Ince's body was cremated, so no autopsy could be performed. And his grieving widow was whisked off to Europe for several months courtesy of Hearst—conveniently away from the reach of the American press. Louella Parsons was also elevated within the Hearst organization, gaining a lifetime contract and the plum assignment as his number-one celebrity gossip columnist, which she parlayed into a notoriously self-serving enterprise. Conspiracy theorists believe that she wrangled the deal with Hearst to buy her silence about the true cause of Ince's death.

Was Ince the victim of an errant gunshot and subsequent cover-up? If anyone in 1920s California had the power to hush witnesses and bend officials to his will in order to get away with murder, it was the super rich and powerful Hearst. But no clear evidence of foul play has emerged after all these decades. Still, the story has persisted and even served as the subject for *The Cat's Meow,* a 2002 film directed by Peter Bogdanovich, which starred Kirsten Dunst as Davies and Cary Elwes as the doomed Ince.

(Do not read this until you have read the previous page!)

1. Thomas Ince's death certificate listed this as the cause of death.
    A. Heart failure
    B. Drowning
    C. Gunshot wound
    D. Aneurysm

2. Thomas Ince died on the ship.
    _____ True
    _____ False

3. Speculation arose about a love triangle between:
    A. William Hearst, Louella Parsons, and Thomas Ince
    B. William Hearst, Marion Davies, and Thomas Ince
    C. William Hearst, Marion Davies, and Charlie Chaplin
    D. Thomas Ince, Marion Davies, and Charlie Chaplin

4. In the movie based off the events, Cary Elwes played this character.
    A. Thomas Ince
    B. William Hearst
    C. Charlie Chaplin
    D. An FBI agent who solved the crime

    Answers on page 189.

Study this picture of the crime scene for 1 minute, then turn the page.

(Do not read this until you have read the previous page!)

Which image exactly matches the picture from the previous page?

1.

2.

3.

4.

Answers on page 189.

A thief hides out in one of the 45 motel rooms listed in the chart below. The motel's in-house detective received a sheet of four clues, signed "The Logical Thief." Using these clues, the detective found the room number within 15 minutes—but by that time, the thief had fled. Can you find the thief's motel room quicker?

1. The second digit is larger than the first.

2. The sum of the digits is less than 9.

3. The first digit is odd, and the second even.

4. The first number is greater than 1.

51	52	53	54	55	56	57	58	59
41	42	43	44	45	46	47	48	49
31	32	33	34	35	36	37	38	39
21	22	23	24	25	26	27	28	29
11	12	13	14	15	16	17	18	19

Answers on page 189.

Every word listed is contained within the group of letters. Words can be found in a straight line horizontally, vertically, or diagonally. They may be read either forward or backward.

THE ANIMAL

THE BARBER

BIG VINNY

BOMP

BOZEY

THE BRAIN

BUGSY

THE CHEESEMAN

THE CLOWN

CRAZY JOE

DAPPER DAN

FAT TONY

FATS

GRIM REAPER

ICEMAN

JIMMY BLUE EYES

KILLER

LEFTY

LOUIE HA HA

THE RIFLEMAN

THE SNAKE

TEFLON DON

VINNY THE CHIN

THE WOLF

```
V F E T H E B R A I N N A O Y D Y F R
W L C F R G O B J I C E M A N N L E F
E O L P T T U F W E T M N A O O B Z G
R U M S J G H A T C V A P T W R F N J
B I L U S I B T T W M B T E A L O E Q
C E B Y A G K S T E I A H B V D D K M
B H E E W I W W S G F T E I N A X A J
C A H A L H C E V N Z H N O P W E N I
N H Q L Y A E I R J T N L P M O B S M
G A E C D H N I D Y Y F E B J Y Y E M
R R M W C N Q U J T E R H Y T H N H Y
I O X E Y B Z F H T D U Z K X M W T B
M V H V L R O E V A S A K R W U O W L
R T N H V F C Z N N R Q U V H S L J U
E X F P P H I Z E C X L Z D H F C I E
A B L O I K A R X Y L A E V K O E Z E
P X L N E L R I E S A M E F G G H E Y
E J L A M I N A E H T N O I T J T D E
R S E C H H M G N P T L V W N Y P Q S
```

157   Answers on page 190.

Read this true crime account, then turn to the next page to test your knowledge.

Some will tell you that people are just born bad, while others think society is responsible. In the case of 24-year-old Murl Daniels, his turn for the worst came from a chance encounter inside an institution meant to rehabilitate him: the Mansfield Reformatory.

In 1948, while serving time at Mansfield Reformatory for a robbery conviction, Murl Daniels was introduced to another inmate, John West, who was incarcerated for stealing an automobile. The two quickly became friends and started discussing all the robberies they could commit together once they were released. According to legend, Daniels and West also made a pact to hunt down and kill all the prison guards and officials they felt had done them wrong.

By July, both Daniels and West had been released. They wasted no time getting started on their new partnership in crime, beginning by holding up Columbus-area bars and taverns. While the two men always carried guns with them, for the first few robberies, they never fired a single shot. That all changed when Daniels and West burst into a Columbus tavern owned by Earl Ambrose and shot him to death during a robbery attempt.

Perhaps it was that first taste of blood that set them off. Regardless, after the Ambrose murder, Daniels and West continued their murderous spree and headed north to Mansfield. It is believed the duo's first target was to be a Mansfield guard named Harris, but they didn't know where he lived. They intended to get the address from Harris's supervisor and the superintendent of the prison's farm, John Niebel. Since Niebel also lived on that farm, Daniels and West knew how to get there.

On the evening of July 21, 1948, Harris and West snuck into the farmhouse and dragged Niebel, his wife, and his 20-year-old daughter from their beds. After forcing the entire family to strip naked, the pair led them out into a field, where all three were shot to death. Daniels and West then fled, abandoning their plan to track down Harris.

The following day, neighbors discovered the bodies of the Niebel family. It didn't take long for authorities to determine that Daniels and West were the men they were looking for. They began the largest manhunt in Ohio history up to that time. Surprisingly, the killers didn't immediately try to flee Ohio. Rather, they only headed as far north as Cleveland, where they continued their rampage, stealing cars and often shooting and killing the owners in the process. Local newspapers quickly got wind of the pair's crime spree, nicknaming them the Mad Dog Killers.

When Daniels and West finally decided to get the heck out of Ohio, it was too late. On July 24, the pair were met by a police roadblock as they closed in on the state line. While Daniels was willing to give up quietly, West would not go down without a fight. He opened fire on the officers lining the roadblock and was finally shot dead. Daniels was arrested without incident, thus ending a two-week killing spree that claimed the lives of six innocent victims.

Daniels was put on trial for the murders of the Niebel family, found guilty on all counts, and sentenced to death. He met the Ohio State Penitentiary electric chair on January 3, 1949. He was only 24 years old.

(Do not read this until you have read the previous page!)

1. West was in prison for this crime when he met Daniels.
   A. Robbery
   B. Stealing an automobile
   C. Murder
   D. Conspiracy

2. Daniels and West were nicknamed this.
   A. The Butchers
   B. The Unrepentent
   C. The Prison Murderers
   D. The Mad Dog Killers

3. This man died in a shootout with police.
   A. Murl Daniels
   B. John West
   C. John Daniels
   D. Murl West

4. The murder of the Niebel family was their first criminal act after prison.
   _____ True
   _____ False

Answers on page 190.

Read this true crime explainer, then turn to the next page to test your knowledge.

What is the difference between a mass murderer and a serial killer?

A mass murderer kills four or more people during a short period of time, usually in one location. In most cases, the murderer has a sudden mental collapse and goes on a rampage, progressing from murder to murder without a break. About half the time, these outbreaks end in suicides or fatal standoffs with the police. Various school shootings over the years have been instances of mass murder. A case in which someone murders his or her entire family is a mass murder. Terrorists are lumped into this category as well, but they also make up a group of their own.

A serial killer usually murders one person at a time (typically a stranger), with a "cooling off" period between each transgression. Unlike mass murderers, serial killers don't suddenly snap one day—they have an ongoing compulsion that drives them to kill, often in very specific ways. Serial killers may even maintain jobs and normal relationships while going to great lengths to conceal their killings. They may resist the urge to kill for long periods, but the compulsion ultimately grows too strong to subjugate. After the third victim, an aspiring killer graduates from plain ol' murderer to bona fide serial killer.

In between these two groups, there are the spree killer and the serial spree killer. A spree killer commits murder in multiple locations over the course of a few days. This is often part of a general crime wave. For example, an escaped convict may kill multiple people, steal cars, and rob a store as he tries to escape the police. As with a mass murderer, a spree killer doesn't plan each murder individually.

The serial spree killer, on the other hand, plans and commits each murder separately, serial-killer style. But he or she doesn't take time off between murders or maintain a double life. One of the best-known examples is the Washington, D.C.-area beltway snipers who killed ten people within three weeks in October 2002.

(Do not read this until you have read the previous page!)

1. Someone who kills two people at once is considered:

    A. A mass murderer

    B. A serial killer

    C. A spree killer

    D. None of the above

2. Serial killers may resist the urge to kill for long periods.

    _____ True

    _____ False

3. Spree killers don't plan each of their murders individually.

    _____ True

    _____ False

4. Mass murders often end in suicide.

    _____ True

    _____ False

          Answers on page 190.

PERFECTION

Cryptograms are messages in substitution code. Break the code to read the message. For example, THE SMART CAT might become FVO QWGDF JGF if **F** is substituted for **T, V** for **H, O** for **E,** and so on.

B CBE EBCZV DFMZHS NLWYYBLV TBM FEZ FG OSZ
AZNZEVBLX DZTZA OSWZRZM FG SWM BNZ. WE 1913,
SZ MOFAZ B GBCFQM MOLWEN FG HLZPWFQM HZBLAM
GLFC B MZBAZV JFU TSWAZ OSZX TZLZ WE OLBEMWO.
BVVWEN WEMQAO OF WEDQLX, SZ LZHABPZV OSZ
HZBLAM TWOS MQNBL PQJZM JZGFLZ MZBAWEN OSZ
JFU BEV AZBRWEN OSZ OSZGO OF JZ VWMPFRZLZV.

Answers on page 190.

Read these accounts, then turn to the next page to test your knowledge.

During the Middle Ages, people believed that animals were legally responsible for their crimes and misdeeds. But punishment was not administered without fair trial. Let's look at a few of these cases.

The year was 1386. In the French city of Falaise, a child was killed and partially devoured by a sow and her six piglets. Locals refused to let such a heinous crime go unpunished. However, rather than killing the sow, they brought her to trial. The pig was dressed in men's clothing, tried for murder, convicted, and hanged from the gallows in the public square.

Porkers weren't the only animals to face trial during medieval times. Bees, snakes, horses, and bulls were also charged with murder. Foxes were charged with theft. Rats were charged with damaging barley. In the early 1700s, Franciscan friars in Brazil brought "white ants" (probably termites) to trial because "the said ants did feloniously burrow beneath the foundation of the monastery and undermine the cellars . . . threatening its total ruin."

The first record of animal trials exists in Athens. More than 2,000 years ago, the Athenians instituted a special court to try murderous objects (such as stones and beams) as well as animals that caused human deaths. They believed that in order to protect moral equilibrium and to prevent the wrath of the Furies, these murders had to be avenged.

Animal trials peaked in the Middle Ages, ranging from the 9th century to as late as the 18th century. During this time, people believed that animals committed crimes against humans and that, like humans, animals were morally and legally responsible for their actions. As a result, animals received the same punishment as humans, ranging from a knock on the head to excommunication or death.

of crimes in Europe's Middle Ages received the same rights under the law as humans, which included a fair trial. Domestic animals were often tried in civil courts and punished individually. Animals that existed in groups (such as weevils, eels, horseflies, locusts, caterpillars, and worms) were usually tried in ecclesiastical courts. They weren't stretched on the rack to extract confessions, nor were they hanged with individual nooses. Instead, they received a group malediction or anathema.

The accused animals were also entitled to legal representation. When the weevils in the French village of St. Julien were accused of threatening the vineyards in 1587, Pierre Rembaud argued in their defense. The innocent weevils should not be blamed, said Rembaud. Rather, the villagers should recognize God's wrath and don sackcloth. The court ruled in favor of the weevils and gave them their own parcel of land.

As for the six little piglets in Falaise? They also must have had good counsel—they were acquitted on the grounds of their youth and their mother's poor example.

Murder wasn't the only crime to carry a death sentence. Often, animals accused of witchcraft or other heinous crimes received similar punishment. In 1474, a cock was burned at the stake in Basel, Switzerland, for the crime of laying an egg. As was widely understood, this could result in the birth of a basilisk, a monster that could wreak havoc in a person's home.

Pigs were often brought to the gallows for infanticide (a perennial problem since 900-pound sows often ran free). A mother pig smothering her infants was most likely an accident, but in those times people saw it as a sign of evil thanks to the Biblical account of the demon-possessed herd at Gadarenes.

Animals had slim hopes for survival when accused of severe crimes. However, there is the amazing account of a jenny that was saved when the parish priest and the citizens signed a certificate that proclaimed her innocence. It stated that they had known the "she-ass" for four years and that "she had always shown herself to be virtuous and well-behaved both at home and abroad and had never given occasion of scandal to anyone."

(Do not read this until you have read the previous page!)

1. The Ancients Greeks put animals on trial.

_____ True

_____ False

2. Animals such as horseflies or locusts were often tried in groups and received group maledictions.

_____ True

_____ False

3. Trials could end in the animal being declared innocent.

_____ True

_____ False

4. In the case at Falaise, the pig was drowned as punishment for murder.

_____ True

_____ False

Answers on page 191

Study this picture of the crime scene for 1 minute, then turn the page.

(Do not read this until you have read the previous page!)

1. The placards marking the bullets show these numbers:

   A. 1, 2, 3

   B. 1, 2, 3, 4

   C. 1, 2, 3, 5

   D. 1, 2, 3, 4, 5

2. The police car's front lights were:

   A. On

   B. Off

3. The police car's siren lights were:

   A. On

   B. Off

4. A knife was found at the scene.

   A. Yes

   B. No

Answers on page 191.

Cryptograms are messages in substitution code. Break the code to read the message. For example, THE SMART CAT might become FVO QWGDF JGF if **F** is substituted for **T, V** for **H, O** for **E,** and so on.

QPU OQINX MIUO QPBQ TPUG BG UFUNBEW KBNRNU TBO OQIEUG JNIF AIOUKPHGU, GBKIEUIG'O THJU (QPIRMP QPUX PBW NUZUGQEX WHSINZUW), QPU UFKUNIN QRNGUW HG WUOKUNBQHIG QI B OIERQHIG QPBQ ZIREW PBSU ZIFU JNIF B FISHU—PU OUQ B QPHUJ QI ZBQZP B QPHUJ. PU QBMMUW URMÈGU JNBGÇIHO SHWIZL JIN QPU AID, B FBG TPI PBW TINCUW BO B OKX BGW HGJINFBGQ JIN QPU KIEHZU. SHWIZL WUJHGHQUEX WHW ZNUBQU QPU JHNOQ WUQUZQHSU DRNUBR HG QPU TINEW; PHO HGJERUGZU IG QPU OZHUGZU IJ WUQUZQHIG BJJUZQUW UBNEX WUQUZQHSU TNHQUNO ORZP BO UWMBN BEEBG KIU BGW BNQPRN ZIGBG WIXEU.

169   Answers on page 191.

Every word listed is contained within the group of letters. Words can be found in a straight line horizontally, vertically, or diagonally. They may be read either forward or backward.

ALEXANDER PEARCE

BOONE HELM

CATHERINE WILSON

DELPHINE LALAURIE

EDME CASTAING

EDWARD RULLOFF

GESCHE GOTTFRIED

HARRY T. HAYWARD

HÉLÈNE JÉGADO

JOHN LYNCH

JOHN WILLIAMS

LIZZIE HALLIDAY

MARTIN DUMOLLARD

MARY BATEMAN

PATTY CANNON

PIERRE FRANÇOIS LACENAIRE

THOMAS NEILL CREAM

STEPHEN RICHARDS

THOMAS GRIFFITHS WAINEWRIGHT

WILLIAM PALMER

```
D N R L K Y P E L I Z Z I E H A L L I D A Y J W U R Y
W O Y C T M E Z D S K X N Y Y G C W B G L Q O C G I G
I S A N V H L A T W F L S Q L R T B M V E X H J L U Z
R L B N W K O E E E A P E H P T J Q O S X T N X M E T
O I C B A D D M P P R R L D O S X P W W A C W G A H U
G W V Q Q K Z C A Z V B D I M V B D L A N Q I A R Q D
O E W H C T U C K S W Y M R W E G X Q O D O L I T S A
A N A E I K I B V X N A F G U Z C I C N E J L C I Z C
J I O C M W G X N H R E Y V B L F A N B R L I E N O Q
L R J W I F S H C Y I U I Z G T L N S J P T A F D Y G
H E D Y B B U N B R X A R L Y J H O G T E H M H U S Q
E H F T X N Y A O G E M M J L K A T F B A I S U M T E
L T I Z L L T U D B V M V P O C R X U F R I W F O E I
E A S G N E W B I C A E L R P A R K X P C S N C L P R
N C L H M B C G N R Z W F A E H Y E U Q E Y C G L H U
E X O A E C L M J I Z O P I P W T A A V Z J V A A E A
J J N D Z F T V P B U L G X P M H E P M T B H H R N L
E F Q P H K Z Y H O W T Y K F L A Y T T C N X S D R A
G E S C H E G O T T F R I E D U Y I H L K D P C V I L
A S M I I E C A B W E K D N B W W J L V U P U P C C E
D F S J T H C D L G C P D P L K A H C L N I T G Z H N
O M L E H E N O O B T L H V K K R F C N I F F E B A I
N O N N A C Y T T A P H L Y C T D O N O H W Q U X R H
L A V O U C E K B W A T N V P H Q T X V F I Q Q I D P
K U Q Y U C I W N V N K E T D A Q M X W J E I T D S L
E R I A N E C A L S I O C N A R F E R R E I P M I C E
T H O M A S G R I F F I T H S W A I N E W R I G H T D
```

Answers on page 192.

ANSWERS

AL CAPONE
(PAGE 4)

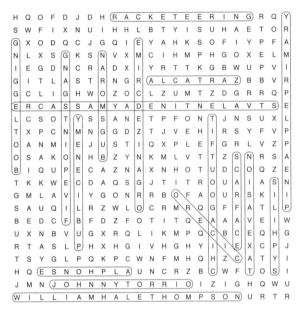

TRIAL OF THE CENTURY (1927 EDITION) (PART II)
(PAGE 8)

1. A. Albert; 2. B. A tie clip with his initials; 3. C. The Blonde Butcher; 4. A. *The Daily News*

CRIMINAL BROTHERS
(PAGE 9)

Jesse and Frank James joined the Quantrill Raiders gang in their teen years and began their lifestyle of bank and train robbery. Jesse's mother Zerelda wrote a book after his death with the dedication: "In Loving Memory of my Beloved Son, Murdered by a Traitor and Coward Whose Name is not Worthy to Appear Here."

TRIAL OF THE CENTURY (1927 EDITION) (PART I)
(PAGE 6)

See part II.

ILLEGAL PETS
(PAGE 10)

Dates	Owners	Streets	Animals
August 4	Edith Estes	Walnut Ave.	skunk
August 5	Iva Ingram	Green Blvd.	bear cub
August 6	Gil Gates	Post St.	cheetah
August 7	Abe Alvarez	Island Rd.	wolf
August 8	Flora Flynn	Kirk Ln.	anaconda

MOTEL HIDEOUT
(PAGE 12)

The thief is in room 14.

OVERHEARD INFORMATION (PART I)
(PAGE 13)

See part II.

OVERHEARD INFORMATION (PART II)
(PAGE 14)

1. D; 2. B; 3. A; 4. C

FIND THE WITNESS
(PAGE 15)

The Winchells live in house B.

STOLEN ART
(PAGE 16)

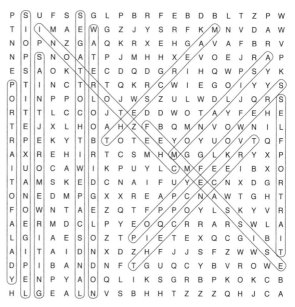

FIND A CLUE ON A RAID
(PAGE 18)

Answers may vary. CLUE, glue, glum, slum, slim, slid, said, RAID

BLUEBEARD IN THE FLESH (PART I)
(PAGE 19)

See part II.

BLUEBEARD IN THE FLESH (PART II)
(PAGE 20)
1. False; 2. A, Arsenic; 3. True; 4. C, 40

SEEN AT THE SCENE (PART I)
(PAGE 21)
See part II.

SEEN AT THE SCENE (PART II)
(PAGE 22)
Picture 1 is a match.

FEMALE BANK ROBBERS (PART I)
(PAGE 23)
See part II.

FEMALE BANK ROBBERS (PART II)
(PAGE 24)
1. B. 5%; 2. A. Parker; 3. D. Machine Gun Molly; 4. C. 1960s

OVERHEARD INFORMATION (PART I)
(PAGE 25)
see part 2

OVERHEARD INFORMATION (PART II)
(PAGE 26)
1. B; 2. C; 3. D; 4. C

MOTEL HIDEOUT
(PAGE 27)
The thief is in room 54.

UNSOLVED MYSTERIES
(PAGE 28)

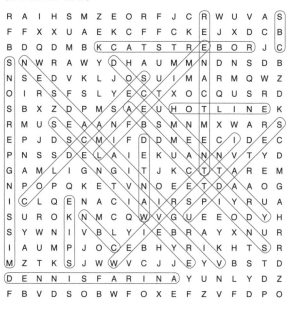

A VENDOR OF DEATH
(PAGE 30)

Italian poisoner Guilia Tofana lived in the 1600s. She developed a poison called Aqua Tofana and sold it to women looking to murder their husbands. When the police came for her, she fled and sought sanctuary in a church; locals grateful for her previous help protected her. Eventually, however, she was arrested and executed, along with her daughter and several other accomplices.

SEEN AT THE SCENE (PART I)
(PAGE 31)
See part II.

SEEN AT THE SCENE (PART II)
(PAGE 32)
Picture 3 is a match.

SEEN AT THE SCENE (PART I)
(PAGE 33)
See part II.

SEEN AT THE SCENE (PART II)
(PAGE 34)
Picture 2 is a match.

OVERHEARD INFORMATION (PART I)
(PAGE 35)
See part II.

ANSWERS

OVERHEARD INFORMATION (PART II)
(PAGE 36)

1. A; 2. B; 3. D; 4. D

MOTEL HIDEOUT
(PAGE 37)

The thief is in room 37.

THE FATTY ARBUCKLE SCANDAL
(PAGE 38)

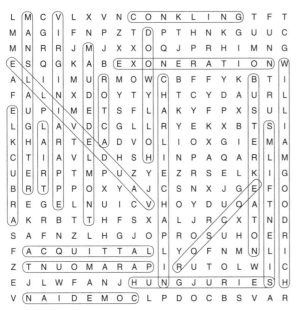

AN ANCIENT TRUE CRIME
(PAGE 40)

Gilles Garnier died in 1573, burned at the stake. A hermit, he was accused of being a werewolf—specifically, of killing and eating four children. He lived in France.

COLD CASE
(PAGE 41)

Answers may vary. COLD, hold, hole, home, come, came, CASE

THE KINGS OF KHAFAR
(PAGE 42)

Years	Kings	Killers	Poisons
1904	Veri'ma	son	arsenic
1921	Kaponi	uncle	hemlock
1938	Taton-on	cousin	oleander
1955	Lilamaku	brother	cyanide
1972	Anjiwat	wife	strychnine

ENTERPRENEURS OF DEATH (PART I)
(PAGE 44)

See part II.

ENTERPRENEURS OF DEATH (PART II)
(PAGE 46)
1. C. A member of the press; 2. C. 1,000; 3. B. Harry Strauss; 4. A. "Buggsy" Goldstein

SEEN AT THE SCENE (PART I)
(PAGE 47)
See part II.

SEEN AT THE SCENE (PART II)
(PAGE 48)
Picture 3 is a match.

FIND THE WITNESS
(PAGE 49)
Rodriguez lives in house D.

MOTEL HIDEOUT
(PAGE 50)
The thief is in room 24.

AKA
(PAGE 51)
1. B, I; 2. C, H; 3. D; 4. F; 5. G; 6. A; 7. E

LIZZIE BORDEN
(PAGE 52)

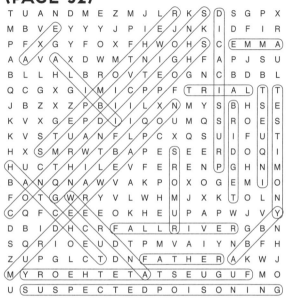

DON'T LEAVE A PRINT
(PAGE 54)
Answers may vary. LEAVE, heave, heavy, heady, heads, hears, heirs, hairs, pairs, paint, PRINT

OVERHEARD INFORMATION (PART I)
(PAGE 55)
see part 2

OVERHEARD INFORMATION (PART II)
(PAGE 56)
1. A; 2. B; 3. C; 4. D

LEWIS HUTCHINSON
(PAGE 57)
This killer was born in Scotland but moved to Jamaica, where he set up an estate called Edinburgh Castle. Travelers who approached the castle too closely tended to disappear. He reportedly tossed his victims into a sinkhole. He was called the Mad Master or the Mad Doctor of Edinburgh. He eventually shot a soldier who had been sent to capture him. He then tried to flee the area, but was caught, tried, and hanged.

THE REAL BONNIE AND CLYDE (PART I)
(PAGE 58)
See part II.

THE REAL BONNIE AND CLYDE (PART II)
(PAGE 60)
1. A. Texas, Louisiana; 2. C. Cut off two toes; 3. False; 4. True

SEEN AT THE SCENE (PART I)
(PAGE 61)
See part II.

SEEN AT THE SCENE (PART II)
(PAGE 62)
Picture 1 is a match.

MOTEL HIDEOUT
(PAGE 63)
The thief is in room 11.

D.B. COOPER
(PAGE 64)

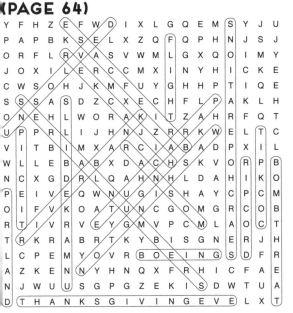

FINDING MURDER
IN THE DICTIONARY
(PART I)
(PAGE 66)
See part II.

FINDING MURDER
IN THE DICTIONARY
(PART II)
(PAGE 68)
1. C. U.S. Civil War; 2. A. Broadmoor Criminal Lunatic Asylum; 3. A. New English Dictionary; 4. A. One person

SEEN AT THE SCENE
(PART I)
(PAGE 69)
See part II.

SEEN AT THE SCENE
(PART II)
(PAGE 70)
1. False; 2. True; 3. False; 4. True

MOTEL HIDEOUT
(PAGE 71)
The thief is in room 48.

PARKING TICKETS
(PAGE 72)

Times	Models	Colors	Locations
10:00am	Nissan	black	Sandy St.
11:00am	Chevrolet	silver	Apple Ave.
12:00pm	Mazda	brown	Tawny Terr.
1:00pm	Honda	green	Raffle Rd.
2:00pm	Toyota	blue	Lantern Ln.

JACK THE RIPPER
(PAGE 74)

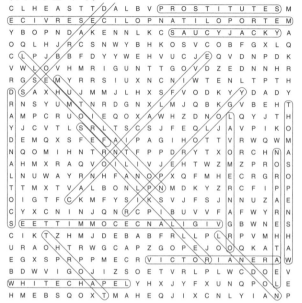

MOTEL HIDEOUT
(PAGE 76)

The thief is in room 19.

OVERHEARD INFORMATION (PART I)
(PAGE 77)

see part 2

OVERHEARD INFORMATION (PART II)
(PAGE 78)

1. A; 2. C; 3. B; 4. D

THE MURDER CASTLE
(PAGE 79)

H. H. Holmes died before he turned 35. In his relatively short life, he committed a number of murders, though the exact number is unknown. It may have been fewer than 10, but it may have numbered more than 100. Holmes was also a bigamist, marrying three different women. Holmes was active at the time of the 1893 World's Fair in Chicago, Illinois. He owned a building to which he lured victims under the guide that it was a hotel; it was later dubbed the Murder Hotel and the Murder Castle for the killings he committed there.

BOOTH'S CO-CONSPIRATORS (PART I)
(PAGE 80)
See part II.

BOOTH'S CO-CONSPIRATORS (PART II)
(PAGE 82)
1. D; 2. B; 3. False; 4. True

FIND THE WITNESS
(PAGE 83)
White lives in house C.

THE "MOST HATED MAN IN THE WORLD"
(PAGE 84)

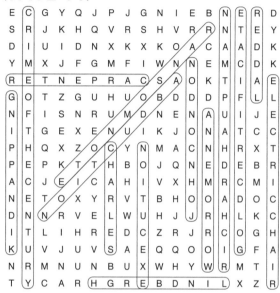

JACK THE RIPPER (PART I)
(PAGE 86)
See part II.

JACK THE RIPPER (PART II)
(PAGE 88)
1. A. Mary Ann Nichols; 2. B. grandson; 3. C. Five; 4. C. The prince's reported child

SEEN AT THE SCENE (PART I)
(PAGE 89)
See part II.

SEEN AT THE SCENE (PART II)
(PAGE 90)
The numbers on the two placards in the back have been swapped.

OVERHEARD INFORMATION (PART I)
(PAGE 91)
see part 2

OVERHEARD INFORMATION (PART II)
(PAGE 92)
1. B; 2. A; 3. B; 4. C

BROTHERS IN CRIME
(PAGE 93)
The Harpe brothers Micajah and Wiley lived in the late 1700s. Micajah was called the "Big Harpe" and his brother the "Little Harpe." They were highwayman and "river pirates," men who preyed on ships. Micajah was killed by a vengeful posse in 1799, while Wiley managed to evade justice until he was caught, tried, and executed in 1804. At the time, he was trying to collect a reward by turning in the head of a fellow criminal.

SHOOT-OUT AT LITTLE BOHEMIA (PART I)
(PAGE 94)
See part II.

SHOOT-OUT AT LITTLE BOHEMIA (PART II)
(PAGE 96)
1. D. 1934; 2. A. Her nephew's birthday party; 3. C. The name of the lodge; 4. True

MOTEL HIDEOUT
(PAGE 97)

The thief is in room 22.

HISTORICAL MURDERERS
(PAGE 98)

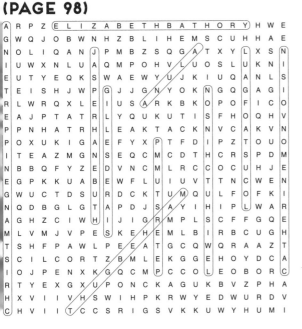

LOST LIBRARY BOOKS
(PAGE 100)

Years	Borrowers	Authors	Titles
1918	Danica	Keith Koch	*Grey Skies*
1931	Angelica	Heddy Heath	*In or Out*
1944	Edith	Jim Joyner	*Just Friends*
1957	Bailey	Nick Norris	*Fine Days*
1970	Charles	Midge Mintz	*High Tide*

MIRANDA WARNING (PART I)
(PAGE 102)

See part II.

MIRANDA WARNING (PART II)
(PAGE 104)

1. D. 1963; 2. C. Fifth Amendment; 3. B. Earl Warren; 4. False

FIND THE WITNESS
(PAGE 105)

Perez lives in house D.

BRAZEN ARMORED CAR HEISTS (PART I)
(PAGE 106)

See part II.

BRAZEN ARMORED CAR HEISTS (PART II)
(PAGE 108)

1. A. Florida; 2. B. About $19 million; 3. D. Mother's Day gifts; 4. True

MOTEL HIDEOUT
(PAGE 109)

The thief is in room 27.

CRIME AND PUNISHMENT (PART I)
(PAGE 110)

See part II.

CRIME AND PUNISHMENT (PART II)
(PAGE 112)

1. B. Drive-in restaurant; 2. D. All of the above; 3. C. 37,500; 4. True

HAN VAN MEEGERAN
(PAGE 113)

This Dutch painter began as an artist of original work, gaining some success. However, his work was sometimes critiqued as derivative and unoriginal. He eventually turned to forgeries, including of Dutch painter Johannes Vermeer. During World War II, one of the forger's paintings ended up in the hands of Nazi Herman Goring. Van Meegeran was arrested after the war for collaboration with the enemy—until he explained that he hadn't sold a real Vermeer, but a forgery. He was given a lesser sentence for fraud, though he died before he served time in prison.

THE BURKE AND HARE MURDERS
(PAGE 114)

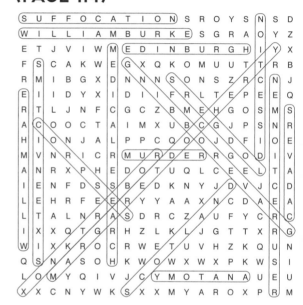

A TANGLED WEB (PART I)
(PAGE 116)

See part II.

A TANGLED WEB (PART II)
(PAGE 118)

1. C. 17 years; 2. A. Arsenic; 3. C. 5; 4. A. Arsenic

SEEN AT THE SCENE (PART I)
(PAGE 119)
See part II.

SEEN AT THE SCENE (PART II)
(PAGE 120)
Picture 2 is a match.

A PROLIFIC FORGER
(PAGE 121)
Tom Keating was born in London in 1914. In his youth, he worked for his family as a painter of houses. Later, after the second world war, he went to college to study art. Although he dropped out, he studied with several art restorers. He then began to forge and sell works of art. However, Keating tended to leave clues in the painting that they were forgeries. He claimed to perceive his forgeries as not so much an intent to defraud but as a way to critique the corruption of the art world. He claimed to have painted more than 2,000 forgeries.

SAMUEL GREEN
(PAGE 122)

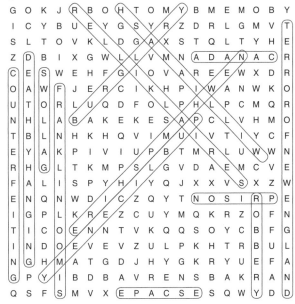

MOTEL HIDEOUT
(PAGE 124)
The thief is in room 51.

OVERHEARD INFORMATION (PART I)
(PAGE 125)
see part 2

185

OVERHEARD INFORMATION (PART II)
(PAGE 126)
1. A; 2. B; 3. B; 4. A

"SUPERMEN" THEY WEREN'T (PART I)
(PAGE 127)
See part II.

"SUPERMEN" THEY WEREN'T (PART II)
(PAGE 128)
1. B. 1920s; 2. A. Loeb's cousin; 3. A. Defense attorney; 4. False

SURVEILLANCE STILL (PART I)
(PAGE 129)
See part II.

SURVEILLANCE STILL (PART II)
(PAGE 130)
Picture 4 is a match.

FIND THE WITNESS
(PAGE 131)
Brown lives in house E.

POLICE DISPATCHER
(PAGE 132)

Times	Officers	Calls	Locations
8:45am	Neville	bank robbery	Midtown
9:30am	Harry	alarm	Downtown
10:15am	Linda	stolen car	Bus. District
11:00am	Jeffrey	trespassing	South End
11:45am	Dale	cat in tree	Uptown
12:30pm	Brenda	accident	North End

TRUE CRIME DOCUMENTARIES
(PAGE 134)

THE BUTCHER AND THE THIEF (PART I)
(PAGE 136)

See part II.

THE BUTCHER AND THE THIEF (PART II)
(PAGE 138)

1. D. 15; 2. B. Boarding house; 3. B. A couple found the body of a victim. 4. False

MOTEL HIDEOUT
(PAGE 139)

The thief is in room 35.

LIZZIE BORDEN DID WHAT? (PART I)
(PAGE 140)

See part II.

LIZZIE BORDEN DID WHAT? (PART II)
(PAGE 142)

1. B. Away from home; 2. C. Prussic acid; 3. True; 4. False

A TOWERING THEFT

(PAGE 143)

In the seventeenth century, a man named Thomas Blood famously tried to steal the crown jewels of England from their tightly guarded location at the Tower of London. Blood first cased the joint; he and a woman pretending to be his wife visited the Tower to see the jewels, ingratiating themselves with the custodian. After several visits, Blood brought some friends to see the jewels. The men then struck down and bound the keeper of the jewels and attempted to abscond with the jewels themselves. It was a messy theft, as the men flattened a crown and filed a scepter in two in order to stash them better beneath clothes. They were caught on attempting to flee. Oddly, Blood was pardoned by the King himself—people speculated that he admired Blood's daring—and even granted an estate.

CRIMES

(PAGE 142)

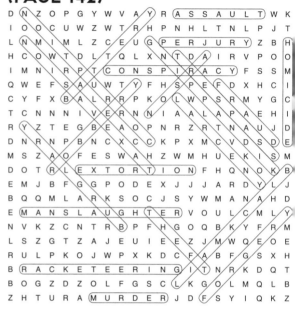

AKA

(PAGE 146)

1. B; 2. F; 3. D; 4. A; 5. E; 6. C

OVERHEARD INFORMATION (PART I)

(PAGE 147)

see part 2

OVERHEARD INFORMATION (PART II)
(PAGE 148)
1. A; 2. B; 3. B; 4. A

HEIST OF THE CENTURY (2003)
(PAGE 149)
What was stolen in the so-called heist of the century? Diamonds, primarily, with some gold and jewelry for good measure. The total came to more than one hundred million dollars. The goods were stolen from the Antwerp World Diamond Centre in Belgium. The thief established himself as a tenant to the building, enabling his access to the vault. He was caught based on a sandwich left near the crime scene. The diamonds, however, were not recovered.

A DEADLY BOATING EXCURSION (PART I)
(PAGE 150)
See part II.

A DEADLY BOATING EXCURSION (PART II)
(PAGE 152)
1. A. Heart failure; 2. False; 3. C. William Hearst, Marion Davies, and Charlie Chaplin; 4. A. Thomas Ince

SEEN AT THE SCENE (PART I)
(PAGE 153)
See part I.

SEEN AT THE SCENE (PART II)
(PAGE 154)
Picture 4 is a match.

MOTEL HIDEOUT
(PAGE 155)
The thief is in room 34.

MAFIA NICKNAMES
(PAGE 156)

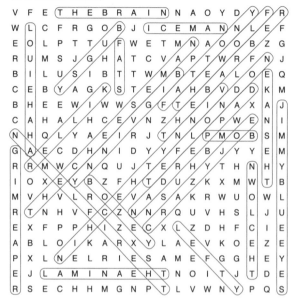

PARTNERS IN MURDER (PART I)
(PAGE 158)
See part II.

PARTNERS IN MURDER (PART II)
(PAGE 160)
1. B. Stealing an automobile; 2. D. The Mad Dog Killers; 3. B. John West; 4. False

MASS MURDERERS VS. SERIAL KILLERS (PART I)
(PAGE 161)
See part II.

MASS MURDERERS VS. SERIAL KILLERS (PART II)
(PAGE 162)
1. D. None of the above; 2. True; 3. True; 4. True

PERFECTION
(PAGE 163)
A man named Joseph Grizzard was one of the legendary jewel thieves of his age. In 1913, he stole a famous string of precious pearls from a sealed box while they were in transit. Adding insult to injury, he replaced the pearls with sugar cubes before sealing the box and leaving the theft to be discovered.

TRUE (ANIMAL) CRIMES (PART I)
(PAGE 164)
See part II.

TRUE (ANIMAL) CRIMES (PART II)
(PAGE 166)

1. True; 2. True; 3. True; 4. False

SEEN AT THE SCENE (PART I)
(PAGE 167)

See part II.

SEEN AT THE SCENE (PART II)
(PAGE 168)

1. C. 1, 2, 3, 5; 2. A. On; 3. Off; 4. B. No

A CRIMINALLY GOOD DETECTIVE
(PAGE 169)

The story goes that when an emerald parure was stolen from Josephine, Napoleon's wife (though they had recently divorced), the emperor turned in desperation to a solution that could have come from a movie—he set a thief to catch a thief. He tagged Eugène François Vidocq for the job, a man who had worked as a spy and informant for the police. Vidocq definitely did create the first detective bureau in the world; his influence on the science of detection affected early detective writers such as Edgar Allan Poe and Arthur Conan Doyle.

MURDERERS OF THE 1800S
(PAGE 171)

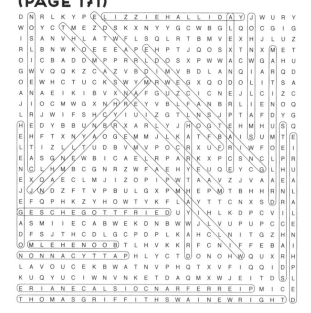